Sophie Laslett

About the Author

Born in London in 1960, FRIEDA HUGHES is a poet, an award-winning painter, and the author of seven books for children. Her poems have appeared in many leading publications, including, among others, *The New Yorker*, *The Paris Review*, *The London Magazine*, *The Spectator*, *The Times*, *Tatler*, *Thumbscrew*, and *Agenda*. Her first collection of poetry, *Wooroloo*, received a Poetry Book Society Special Commendation.

Stonepicker

&

The Book of Mirrors

Also by Frieda Hughes

Stonepicker

&

The Book of Mirrors

POEMS

FRIEDA HUGHES

HARPER  PERENNIAL

NEW YORK • LONDON • TORONTO • SYDNEY • NEW DELHI • AUCKLAND

HARPER ● PERENNIAL

Stonepicker was originally published in Great Britain in 2001 by Bloodaxe Books Ltd.

HarperCollins books may be purchased for educational, business, or sales promotional use. For information please write: Special Markets Department, HarperCollins Publishers, 10 East 53rd Street, New York, NY 10022.

FIRST EDITION

Designed by Justin Dodd

Library of Congress Cataloging-in-Publication Data

Hughes, Frieda.
    Stonepicker and the book of mirrors / Frieda Hughes.—
1st Harper Perennial ed.
      p. cm.
    ISBN 978-0-06-056452-0
    I. Hughes, Frieda. Book of mirrors. II. Title.
PR6058.U347S76 2009
821'.914—dc22   2008045055

09 10 11 12 13 OV/RRD 10 9 8 7 6 5 4 3 2 1

Contents

STONEPICKER

Stonepicker

In memory of my father

Stonepicker

She is scooped out and bow-like,
As if her string
Has been drawn tight.

But really, she is
Plucking stones from the dirt
For her shoulder bag.

It is her dead albatross,
Her cross, her choice,
In it lie her weapons.

Each granite sphere
Or sea-worn flint
Has weight against your sin,

You cannot win.
She calls you close,
But not to let you in, only

For a better aim.

Playground

They were practicing themselves,
Trying out their little fists.
But a punch was nothing new,
It did not have that resounding shock
Of being just invented.

Big girl shook her short hair.
Hot and wretched
She was boiled in her skin
And might unpeel
At any moment.

Her blue wool and gray skirt
Were dragged and twisted round
Her fleshy mountains, and
Small girl laughed
As agile as a goat, and wide-eyed,

Using words that stuck
Like gum on shoes,
Better than a fist and leave a bruise,
And all the legs of little boys
Like bars, and all their noise

Filling up the big girl's head
With memories of ridicule
That would repeat again, again,
For years inside her brain. She knew
One thing must stop it now

Or face it every day at school.
She watched the other girl, mouth wide,

Laugh and point, no matter
How she cried. Her idea was simple;
Take the laugh away.

The small girl didn't scream at first, until
Her bloody lump of thigh
Was bitten out and left.
No more than a mouthful, it silenced laughter
Among the children in the playground

Long after.

Soldier

There are different kinds of war.
In one, a nineteen-year-old girl
Steps aside in the park
For a pregnant woman. She slips
On mud and sodden grass.
Arms out for a fall, her wrists crack
Like two pencils, in unison
With an elbow and an ankle.

The ambulance arrives. Her hands
Are gently wiped to clean
Dog shit from between
Her fingers. Then
Her face is wiped of blood
Where her forehead hit,
And her tears are wiped
With a cloth of blood and shit.

By the time her wrists have healed,
Her eyes are empty. Toxocara
Has crept in, through the cloth of kindness,
Of ignorance, through the skin
Of her corneas. Forty-three operations,
One for a metal heartbeat,
And she is twenty-six today, on a train,
Telling two strangers how

She finds her own dog's shit now,
With the animal's nose, a rubber glove
And a plastic bag. Her words negotiate filth,
As her hands do. A lavatory is where
She cleans each plastic rim

And unseen bit of porcelain
Just to have a pee; her mind's eye
As sharp as her nose for a smell.

Her black dog takes two seats.
He's earned it. His rump
Is dented like tin
Where a knife was stuck in
When she was mugged
For her white stick and
A bag of wet-wipes.

Once, she believed in God.
Now she believes she is being taken
A piece at a time.
All she wants back
Are the birthday flowers from her luggage,
Put on the wrong train
By someone with eyes, who could see.

Visitants

Trees crabbed in their leaves,
Bundled black like old women.
Hunchbacked and planted,
Breathless,
They waited for sound.

Houses, subsiding like three-story
Headstones in a burial ground,
Were blind to the street;
Their windows and doors
Shut like mouths against noise.

And it came.
Hauling its body of notes
Through the night air,
It came. Dragging its throat behind
Like invisible rope, it came.

When it arrived, fixed as I was
Like a camera, I could picture nothing.
The screech repeated as if
To pick itself out and
Hold itself up for a look, at nothing.

For a year, the study window
Was my waiting eye
For the dying goose, or a cat
Beneath a slowly rolling truck;
Anything that could make that cry.

Until one night, my car
Opened up a mouth beneath its windpipe

And scraped asphalt with that same howl;
A bloody-ended, shrill stretch of raw meat,
And no murder.

Winter-bushed and city-blackened, two foxes
Scrambled from the wheel arch.
Baiting each other like lovers,
They collected their noise.
It untangled between them like a joke.

Stones

These earth-jewels are not dumb.
The diamond ones have life
In a woman's eye, and the black hole

Of a tooth in the mouth
Of a man, with a man's fingers
Fingering his molars. It might

Just make it, if it can quiet
Its bright, compacted soul
In its drill-hole.

And dolerite is the Russian doll
Of the desert. Each cracked egg
Is stripped, a year at a time

As each boulder exfoliates its onion layers,
Leaving only a large marble that I will
Thread on my necklace.

Their unpeelings rock in the wilderness, each
Wanting to be a cup for water.
And bloody and rough at the roadside

Are the garnets. Like tongue-warts,
Raw from the mouth of the earth,
They have a whole life

In their little red bodies
If you listen. Not to find a heal
For a wound, or an unpressing

Of a cerebral cortex, or an answer
To a question for the Gods.
Just to hear them.

The Outfit

Long black sat there, bored on the bones beneath,
Idle over the knees, and flat
Against the back beneath short red.

Short red shifted her sleeves a bit
And cried: "It wasn't like this last time!"
Long black sighed. This stillness was wounding.

Last time, neat little weave
That stroked ankles
Had drunk a lot, and tottered.

Black and red had plotted
To take gray wool two-piece to bed,
And succeeded. But tonight, there was nothing doing.

Early at home, they were cupboard-hung
Like little skins. Breathless,
And waiting to be made interesting.

Sisyphus

Dead, she is piled on his back
For the river crossing.

Before, he rolled his stone
Up the mountain while
His wife watched. And then
They watched it roll down again.
It defied him. Now he is
Carrying his wife's carcass.

He reaches the riverbank. Mud
Is thick at his ankles.
Her body stinks from
The buckle of his shoulders,
But the gathered crowd
Will not land him. They stand,
Bank-bound, their words
Sharp like swords, and hold him off.

Slowly, current tugging at his
Bent knees, he turns. Slowly,
He wades back. But they are
Waiting there too, tongues pointed
Like knives. And his wife
Is weighing heavy for her burial.

He turns again.

Fear

He sits on the bed-end, my black foot
Foul-mouth friend. Breath like hot bitumen,
His smile is tangled in those rotten teeth,
His hand upon my ankle like a clamp.

He, heavy jailer, holds me for tomorrow
When they cut out the pain,
Take away the lost flesh like the secret body
Of a dead cat wanting burial, and stitch me back again.

I have made him up of my own mud and clay and blood.
I stapled him together. Gave him life.
He is the only one to touch, and sit, and wait with me,
In my dark, in my room, until it's time.

Dr Shipman

God is a doctor. His secret adores him, as close
To his skin as his beard — hedge-cut
To hide all but his letterbox — and his eyes,
Counting down corpses on his abacus
Ten at a time.

The strength in his poisoned needle
Adds inches to him. His power to take,
Or to leave until later,
Must be the joke that splits apart
His foliage to laugh.

Weeping relatives make him
Their Wailing Wall and he watches,
All death certificates and consternation,
From the superior vantage point
Of his mounting body count.

God, undiscovered in his disguise,
Plans his afternoons so death
Is between lunch and dinner,
Like a snack; a little something
That feeds his empty hole.

When God is found out for being
Someone else, he is thrown into jail.
But he still thinks he's God as long
As he holds the answer to the question.
God locks his tongue in a box, and swallows it.

The Wound

She carries her wound,
It is carefully disguised
Beneath her underclothes.
It is still bleeding.

It is her mother's fault,
When her mother imagines
Her child might not be
Blameless.

It is her father's fault,
For not having a hole
Like hers, so
Not understanding.

It is her husband's fault,
For wanting
To stop up her pain
And the pain, stopping.

Black Cockatoos

The girls are calling.
One with an eye for me
Rolls in her sky
And lets out a cry
That knots cat hair.
Airborne widows,
Their feathers skip fences.
Under armpit
They bring the bush-heat,
And in their breath
Is the red dirt
Where their wings will fold
When they fall.

The Little War

Victim has turned on killer and
The two of them are arguing
Over a television. Killer took it
When the killing started, but somehow
Victim didn't die;
He came home to find
The contents of his house
Had moved across the street.
Now he wants his television back,
And his fridge, and his
Electric cooker but
No one has pointed out
That the power is down
And the generators are in the hands
Of the Russians again. All he knows is
That his fridge still wears
The alphabet magnets brought home
For his dead son. They hold
The last scrap of his wife's face,
Torn, and left beneath
The letter "S" and
He is prepared to kill for it.

Communion

Ten years old, she was asleep. Dreaming,
She was dragged from the folds
That clasped her like a ring stone,

And sat up.

Her head refused to release
The people in it, rolling on her shoulders
With the weight of them.

A face
Was thrust into her face.
An urgent, unlikely face,

Not a house-face.
She must dislodge sleep to see it,
It might never come again.

Her bald eyes struggled for it,
Wanting focus for
A fixing-point.

Ears. He had big ears.
And eyes astonished as her own,
That stared back, unblinking.

Fox met her nose to nose,
So close, his coal-tip was too soon
For a sharp edge.

She wanted to climb inside
His black holes, and stroke
His terror down.

Orphan four-legs, off to find a home,
Brought in to be shown
Just once.

She was still
Embedded in him as
He was carried to the door.

Incision

He calls her.
Not with his mouth open
And an audible cry,
But with the two wet lips
Of his surgeon's incision,

As if he had given birth
To his daughter
From his own sliced belly
And left that mouth open,
Waiting for an answer.

And there she is,
Bearing a scar
From the same procedure;
Tiger stripe for tiger stripe.

In his held breath
Is the nurse with her hand
On the mouthpiece of a phone,
Where his brother sits
Gagged by her fingers.

Tiger weeps when spear
Parts his second and third ribs,
But understands anyway. Then dies.
Maybe this new mouth
Will have a real shout.

The sound will escape from the stitches
And be heard in the blood
As it dries on the sheets.
A sudden, loud red scream
When the covers are stripped.

Beauty 1

Picked brows and puckered mouth,
Pumped up with belly fat, and belly
Sucked in through a tube,
Through a hole in you.

The look has become the life. The bed edge
Is pushed further beneath the knife.
A little tuck, a little cut, are not a lot
From last time. Seventh, eighth or ninth time.

But the face is not the one you wore before
Your seventeenth birthday. Men hold it
In their hands, your lips, like petals,
Curling with tattoo. You have made

A thing that only is, if someone looks,
And looks, and looks.

Beauty 2

Italian waiter poured the water
As I waited. The seat opposite
Marking me out as if
I were naked.

I watched the couple
Led to the table beside me.
He had a face that
Thirteen-year-old girls

Would-color copy twenty times
And pin to their walls, his many eyes
Like swords, polishing on their new breasts. She
Was the surprise. A nothing face.

Not bulbous, nor lumpy,
Nor scarred, nor strange at all. But blank
And plain beneath her mouse-cap of hair.
Hand-held, his looks dwarfed her.

She smiled. There was this
Pulling back of skin to let in light.
Her voice was a pounding river, where he swam
Over the perfect white stones of her teeth.

Her fingers were tiger lilies, dancing.
She was illuminated
Like colored glass, and he
Was kneeling at her window.

The Bird Cage

It is bright and gold, ring hold
At the top, for a chain.
A little girl is caught in its bars
As surely as the toy bird.

Each of them, perch-bound. One looking out,
The other peering in, but trapped
By those green and blue feathers and
The bead of a dead eye.

Not given to her, she must watch
Another child carry the canary
To a hot spot on the radiator
For its trick.

And there it is left in the rising air.
The bird shudders as if life has just been
Forced back through its yellow beak
And into its small mechanical breast.

Its wings open, its tail spreads
And suddenly it is singing:
"I should have been yours,
I should have been yours."

Leaving

On Wednesday, the fridge
And the bed left together
With a woman
In high, black heels.

The table and chairs
Went off with a man
Who came for the TV
And six extension leads.

Hippies in a combi bought the hi-fi,
And the valley turned out
For the garage sale and
A cordless phone.

We were throwing the anchors off!
If someone would only
Steal the car
We could go.

Phone Call

She's done it again.
Hardly ever a man would call
This way. Even
A stealer of days would be
More of a javelin thrower.

But her voice is all warm
For the dog in you,
Word-beaten, daring to play again,
With the sucking child
And its rattle of scream.

She opens her mouth,
As big as the door of her house,
To let you in
With your toothpick
For the bits in her teeth,

And the pounding of train
From the back of her tongue,
Through the eye of the telephone.
And when she is done,
She is already calling again.

Warrior

Behind the boy's eyes
Are all the little devils. And you,
You, with your mask over
Everything in front of you,
Want to pound him beneath
The feet you have borrowed.
Picked up with the uniform,
Your boots have pride in being matched
With many others.
They want things. As you
Bring down your cudgel upon
Something you thought would not
Crack that way, all your brothers
Are murdered. And when
You are driven home, driven like
The cattle you killed, like
The people you buried,
There is a man with boots
Towering above, brandishing
His own mace. He is
Reclaiming his place, but now
You are nothing to him either.

Lucky Stone

As near a ball as an eye,
Its dull black as heavy as gold
Was hot in my hand,
I made it my luck.

At a touch all the time,
Pocket polished and as special
As a gift outside birthdays,
It turned in its dark, on its axis.

Stone, by nature, being stone,
Sidled up to the threads that held it.
Smooth though it was, and toothless,
It somehow had teeth.

My hand in my pocket
Found it empty. Suddenly,
Stunned, my brain
Fell to the bucket-bottom.

All my luck had passed
Through a hole. Street-scattered
Among miles of pavement
It was gone.

For days I paced each turn
I'd made, each detour.
Nothing else was as sacred
As my lost luck.

I found a smooth brown pebble
Almost round. A thing that stood out

From the baked dirt.
I slipped it into my pocket.

I was going to find it some friends, but
Nothing would be given my luck again.
It would sit among many, and I
Would give it no importance at all.

Sunset for Ros

Sky broadens her grin.
We grow old beneath her.
Ever-returning to begin,
She must watch with a laugh.
Her seams and trenches,
Fresh from the furnace
In which they have rolled and flared,
Come back to burn again. Her light
Picks out our surface, and illuminates
Each new furrow upon
Our waning faces.

She takes our last breath
From the dirt of the day,
And ignites it above deserts,
Where stones look back
At their birth mother, blazing.

Myra Painting

Myra, Myra on the wall,
Hung at last to please us all.
The little hands that painted you
Thought it a good game
To pick out your face in its frame,
And fill it in with their fingers.

In your own art, your skill is still
Buried with the children. Little unfound bodies,
Stuck inside your casing like you
Nailed down their mothers, hammering them in.
When the passerby squeezed out
His fountain pen, his was the laugh.

All that is left are mirrors of ink,
Like black pennies drying
Beneath your vacant lot. Outlined
In a square of white tape, like taping
The fallen body, they are a new installation,
And you have gone to be restored.

Drinker

In the morning
We were friends,
Showing off
Our broken pieces.

We read them like rune stones.
You saw men in mine,
Goldfish in my aquarium, all wanting air
And fighting for freedom.

You saw my canvases unroll
Like open wounds,
And the words of poetry
Spill salt on the bloody parts.

But your stones were heavier;
Their haul of unmade phone calls,
Unbuilt houses, and an ex-wife
With your end in mind, dragged.

Your stones rocked in alcohol, your
Other man bottomed out in your glass
As the food toppled
From your falling plate.

I watched your other person
Leave his head on the table
Like a handbag,
And knew I was too late.

Driver

One day, she will pick this up.
Maybe she will remember
Her silver Volvo station wagon
And her silent husband and
Her nine-year-old daughter
Crouched in the back seat,
With a boot full of plants and duvets,
And boxes of weekend CDs.

The girl's face is book-open
In the sound of our horn,
As her mother drives
The silver skin of her
Daughter's chariot
At our pale blue.

And me, with my body wondering
Which wounds to wear this time, and she
With her face in the window, loud about
Wanting our place.
She was aiming her bullet
At our noise —
The only thing that caught her
From falling, and she,
Still wanting to drop.

Hospital Waiting Room

Chipped from outback mud
With a pick and mattock,
All his little parts baked together,
His skin of leather
As dug out as gullies.

His broken arm has brought him in
From the oven, his splintered limb
Tied up in the sling of a tea towel. Pain
Pins him to his chair, as if
He has been harpooned in.

The watch upon his wrist
Ticks off its digital seconds.
Hidden in the blue and white check
Of his kitchen cloth, it is
A little bomb waiting to go off.

At three o'clock we are woken,
Our stupor broken. The screeches
Of his sudden alarm have reached
Into the room's sky,
Pointing him out
Like the arrows of wind vanes.

He suppresses his cry, his tears
Funnel into his hide
Like rain in a creek bed.
This bushman beats desert to squeeze
Water from a branch
And a plastic bag,

But cannot gag the five-dollar clock
That straps his broken wing.

His other hand cannot help;
He is thumping the watch
With a cut-off stump and a bit of an elbow,
Three o'clock, three o'clock, three o'clock,
But his melon-end can't make it stop,
And his left hand hangs helpless
Beneath the watch band.

The large woman beside him
Unfolds, her fat forefinger
Leads her eye to the button
That switches him off,
And, for the first time,
His face unbuckles and opens
Just for her.

Landmines

The legs are waiting.
There must be places in Heaven
Where they are stacked fifteen deep,
Along with fingers and arms
From industrial accidents,
All waiting for their bodies to die
And come to find them.

I may meet up with
My womb again,
And a foot of colon that was severed
At its two ends
To become a worm in an Elysian field.

But every day I walk forward
I do not have to know
That my legs have gone on ahead.

Mother

Three, like stones, her children lay
Smooth, round and heavy in her lap, her little gods.
Kept her fearful and still, her hair pulled out
Thick by roots, blood made,
When he asked a question.
Wrist skin twisted black
Each bone a pivot
If she turned her back.

Sharply dragged, her pain was silent
For the heads she cradled.
But his white powder had a loud, hard voice,
Broke those spheres like glass.
Their shattered faces were perfect moons
A moment before his blunt language
Beat out their edges, and he made them
Wrong forever.

The Dying Room

Mother, father, no child,
Made the space between them
Into a hard thing;
A boulder in the bedroom, washed clean
Where they cried. Secretly, and separate.
Each afraid of the other.
Of their invisible baby.
That rock, their burden, should have been a daughter.

And in the dying room, the children gather.
Where death does not need the language,
But picks his nails and cleans his nostrils
With shin bones small enough to knit with.
He knows they will come easily,
Because the cold seek warmth,
And even in his rot and tatters
He wants them most.

Dressed meat, their moons shine.
Tiny girls, not to know
Why brother lived. Never loved,
They grate until they stop,
Little clocks all run out and empty.
They clatter in their graves like hollow tins
And mother, father, no child,
Polish up their stone again.

Crocodiles

Like squeaky toys, their noise
Makes children coo. Their little eyes
Like balls of wide surprise
Are bugged for mother with
Her mouth of nails. And she,
With limbs like trees
And skin of knotted bark,
And weighing all a ton,
Collects her little ones.
Pouch-rocked in her throat,
She sets them free again
In water, with a tongue
As gentle as fingers.

The Party

They are all out
For the Golden Fleece.
Theseus and Ulysses have found
Carmen Miranda, and hope
They have been recognized.

Hamlet is winding his mother's braid
Around his wrist. Like a watch,
It gives up time.
There is a dark woman
Tapping her fingers on a cold radiator.

She knows who they are. She calculates
Their height and width, she is
Assembling their boxes
And taking photographs,
Until they are all identified.

My Face

As I sleep, other people
Wear my face. It is still
Worn-out when I collect it
From the bathroom mirror
In the morning.

I haven't dared a surgeon yet,
To pick off the lines and
Cast adrift the boats
Of my eyes and nose
And mouth.

But in the forty years
That I have seen them all afloat
Without a cord or chain
To anchor them between my ears,
Above my chin and throat,

My skin spiders and flesh mites
Have been knitting up each
Facial twitch and scratch. They even caught
The creases from my first laugh
When I spilled out of the womb.

Longest worked on, it must
Run the deepest. A straight rope
From voice box to navel. And if the line
Is taut enough, you will hear
It still plays the same note.

Oracle

Only a hole in the wall,
Where fingers have polished
The sill of the voice that speaks
From the gut of your boulder,
And begged for an answer.

The answer stands there, bald
And featherless, on your bottom lip.
It is not always beautiful.
It does not look the way
They think it should.

It opens up the mouth in its
Fleshy mass, in the door of
Your mouth, and the answer
Screeches.
Man bends for his first stone.

Man Starving

The Saturday supplement had been stacked
And left. No one
Would pick it up and place
That man's face beneath their arm.

His black eyes rattled at the back
Of his deep burrows. Their whites
Were wounds in the newsprint.
They leapt up and got you.

He was four-legged like a dog, but
Not from having lost something;
His bones would snap
If he tried to upright his sticks.

His skull smiled up through skin;
Full lips of flesh
Had shriveled and dried like worms,
His teeth were constantly naked.

And the cameraman, without words,
Had picked him up in his lens
And printed him out, over and over again.
We could almost hear him weeping.

Lunch

You sharpen me like a pencil,
Lighting matches just to burn them out.
Hiding your mud feet beneath the table,
You watch the children die in my face.
I see your hair is grayer now,
I have missed pieces of you.
Remember not to show your holes
Or I am ferret in your earth.
But now I see your face is cleared like water,
Filtered through the stones you give
For me to throw and make
The circles on your surface.
We collect our lost parts.
Between us, they polish like opals.

The Lady M

Her gold is gone now. Gotten old,
She has fallen in on her hard white cage.
Bone-dangled and clattering,

Her face is cut sideways and smiles.
She is my mother-eater, she has cheated me of love.
Dry as a split gourd

She meets me like a relative, a lover even.
But her face has drawn its pale curtains on
The pits that bog it, and

Her eyes are closed.
Their black coals are only painted on
Her hollow doll. She herself has gone.

Jezebel

She must imprint him,
She is screaming at the door
To be let in.

One time, she must have him.
Maybe twice, to tattoo his elements
To her uneventful skin.

His stain on the folds of her membrane,
Her Turin shroud,
Could lose him his name.

Added to the others
He will flesh her out. She is nothing
Except through her lovers.

Is he ever going to let her in?

Down on her luck
Jezebel is counting her conquests.
Unknown to them
They have fallen.
She is thinking of selling them off.

She combs her hair and
Applies rouge. Some of them
Are women.

Jezebel's head
Has been severed
By a cart wheel. It rolls off,
Followed by dogs and children.

Her body will pack
Into a small bag.
Every broken bone
Another hinge.

"Am I not beautiful?" she cries,
Her last sentence whispered
From her blunt neck-end
Like the whistle of a hollow reed.

A passing woman bends over the open mouth
And fills it with dirt.
"Quiet, now," she says,
"Or someone will hear you."

Endometriosis

It crawls up through the groin.
Nail hooks pick out steps in soft red,
Seeking places to implant
Like a cat, screaming and curious,
Trapped, too fat with feeding
To get out through the way in.

It takes root and flowers, its bloody petals
Falling where no wind blows to rid the earth-flesh
Of the shedding velvet, that clogs and gags.
The claw-roots run too deep to peel
From the hollows of the inside,
It must be made hungry to die.

The only answer is to steal its food bowl
And cut out the unborn children.

Laugh

Pack animals
Make their food funny.
Hunger hesitates. They watch
What is left on the leg
Still walk, wearing its open wounds.

What hangs from the shoulder
Is a shorter skin, teats
Or testicles dangling, bald,
And bare to air. Bloodied, even,
But left as bobbing ornaments. And there,

Heaving with mateship, nursing
Swollen bellies from another meal,
The beasts lie grassed and steaming.
They watch their food perform
The little dance it does,

Gathering up its fleshy pieces
Like torn petticoats,
To take its stumble and cakefoot
And leave their table, wanting time
To heal.

The Writer's Leg

His body parts knew better
What his talent was. Contentedly, they stretched,
Grew, and waited, growing hairs.

But he was a boy then, and the blood
That pumped him like a piston never let him sit
Long enough to find it.

His arms and legs drew lots to see
Which one would win the right
To let him know and make him listen.

"Not me!" his right arm cried, "he needs me
For his very purpose, my fingers dance,
Their music is the thing we fight for."

"Nor me!" his left arm cried. "As you can see,
I am the balance for all those computer keys.
Without my digits, he does not add up!"

The legs met each other at the knee,
And conferred. They decided on skates.
The first to give in, fall off, or buckle

Would find itself free
To make this boy listen to his head
Above the sound of his own feet, running.

The blind car drove backwards
And hit him hard, so he noticed.
Left him lying there, broken.

His left leg apologized from its
Stitched skin and splinters
For not giving the right leg a proper chance.

Fresh and bloody from its third operation,
Its mouths grinned up at the head and said,
"Now sit and write something.

Where others use a pencil,
You have me. I am your gift,
So use me wisely."

The San Francisco Fire

The Forty-Niners played the fire
At the Candlestick stadium.

The men were on the field
When the plane flew over,
Tail trailing flag advertising a sale.
And the oval skylight was shut as if
Night had clamped it.

So many people with radios
Now switched them on. Watched
The game at the same time
They heard the flames on interview.
Eucalyptus burns best, and the hotel exploded.

The commentary took trees down, ten at a time.
Someone scored a touchdown,
And we knew the people leaving
Were homeless already.
Then came the slow, black snow

With their furniture in it.
And their toys and their photographs,
The water from their swimming pools
And everything in the garden shed.
The crowd cheered. The fire won.

And we walked to our cars in our hundreds,
With the black dust of burned homes
Thick on our chests and shoulders,
In our hair and on our forearms.
We carried the shadow as one.

Salmon

The boy stood, adolescent
In the river gravel, holding
His dead salmon. Its eyes
Begged up at him with clouds in them
And his own eye.

By degrees, he sank. His ankles
Were disappearing and still
The fish lay cold in his palms.
The gravel pebbled against his
Soft, white man-flesh, and in it
Rolled a hundred nested embryos
And he, still clutching the father,
The carcass.

Portrait

Blind, she is painted empty.
Her hollow vessel clatters like a seedpod
Wanting water and a stem to see with.

On the still beach of her face
All her creatures are stuck
In the oil of her shoreline.

Beneath the rocks of her shoulders
Are the mountainous happenings
That molded her.

And in her voice lies her landscape,
Pitted with caves
Of secret wishes for sight,

Beneath the trees of her fingers
Whose roots touch everything,
Bringing everything back

To her black holes.
Had she been put to music
We would have seen her.

Beetle

The little beetle curls his mouse
Into a basket. Tucking in paws,
And tying in the tail.

The mouse is amenable
By way of being dead
From a beetle-bite.

The beetle burrows into
The soft center of mouse-belly,
And lays out her embryos like jewels.

Squirming with the separation of cells,
They grow, split and feed on their casket,
Becoming maggots.

They hollow out their bloody stink-nest
Of dead flesh, which still wears
Its mouse face,

Fattening to fall, and become beetles again.
The first ones out
Get to eat their brothers and sisters.

The Other Amy

She has a secret.

She has nursed it for years.
It has grown up inside her
Like a tree, each branch
Fingered into her blood vessels
As if feeding her,
But she feeds it.

Every morning,
Like a dependent plant,
It receives water.
Every morning
She repeats to it
Her thoughts.

Quietly, she has been
Building her root map
A finger's inch at a time.
If only they knew,
It would shut their open faces
Like doors.

Left Luggage

He was born like a box,
Put together with sides
Of mother and father and
Everyone trying to read
The label of contents.

For a long time he looked after
Each of his occasions, even
That moment when his wife left him.
It was hung from a hook
On one of his walls.

He used to stand inside himself
Sometimes, and have a look.
Dangling in his gallery, it rather
Overshadowed his smaller memory of
Their meeting at the fishmongers.

Between their beginning and end
Was a Nepalese mountain,
The heal for a scar from a straw-jump;
A hidden spike,
And drinks at six weddings.

It was easier just to smell fish
And forget her.
Even his brother's first bike
That he stole, was parked
Up against the punishment.

The day came when all the weight
Of a sumo was accommodated in his frame.
He no longer rattled with expectation.
His digestion was slow, and his belly dragged.
Something must be shed, to move him on.

His internal shelf was weighted down
By his book of self,
Everything was written in.
For weeks, he fingered his
Own pages, trying to work out

What to lose and what to keep,
And what to look at longer.
He read himself over.
Finally, when he had remembered everything,
He got up for a cup of coffee.

Leaving all his chapters
On a park bench
He realized that
He didn't have to go
Back for them.

Silence

If I am silent for long,
Maybe twenty minutes, you will
Fill that quiet with the sound
Of your own traffic, a dog bark,
And the voices of all the people
That inhabit your mind and
Make up your memory:

Your several brothers and sisters
Sitting in an elm tree,
The branches cracking beneath their
Gathered weight like hot fat;
The two wash-hanging mothers
Tossing their words like sock-balls
To and fro, across the fences at the back,
And the first and last partners
You ever made love with.

By the time I speak again,
You may no longer believe me.

If I am silent for years,
You may even bear my children,
Marry my husbands and mourn
The death of my parents. You could
Chop trees from my hillside,
Imagine the smell of my lilies, and complain
My shoes do not consider your feet at all.

If I never speak,
You could invent me completely.

Bagman

The cloth is torn
And stripped, and laid
Like splints along his legs,
Tied with string
To keep him in.

He is heaped. A sack
Of spilling clothes, all rubbished,
That rise and fall with sleep.
And in the rain, his fraying ends
Struggle to escape their knots and twists,
The man inside his chrysalis.

The Secret

She was desperate to know,
And I so longed to tell her.
The words rolled in my mouth
Like sour little beads. Lemon seeds,
Waiting for the spike of her needle to find
The holes in them, and my tongue.

A right word would unwrap
The secret like a bloody gift,
Bought over someone else's body.
I didn't give it. But it was
Pointed out by all my efforts
Not to tell.

Will she, who understands,
Become now dangerous?
Or is she after all,
A proper keeper of
My sullen jewel?

Breasts

Scarred beneath their bags
Of heavy silicone,
They were mountains,
Shored up and sharpened,
A handful of the mind's mud
At a time. Those breasts

Weren't for a limp sweater,
Or a bra size more than
Two saucers. Those breasts
Had purpose. Men's eyes
Would unpage magazines
For a sight of them.

Melissa was no longer
Required to speak.
Her breasts could talk.
They had a language
And everyone
Understood.

When at last she made the photo shoot,
She gently placed her breasts
Of shiny plastic flesh
Upon the table for
The cameraman,
And left.

Fox Head

Stunned, it was listening
To two men talk. Goggling,
Its eyes, glass-beaded, popped,
And its ears were pricked
For every word. Like a telephone

Pretending it could hear,
The cord-end
Severed,
This head's neck
Wasn't going anywhere.

The Signature

One for you, one for me,
The books are being
Divided between us. Leftovers
From a library where, at night
In the dark, or between
Dinner downstairs and the bathroom,
Sticky fingers would find
Whole volumes stuck to them.

Each book is opened, and there
She has written her name. A mother
For you, a mother for me,
Another for you, another for me,
And suddenly, a small square
Cut from the page corner where
Her ink had dried.

Perhaps the coat pocket was
Too small for the whole story,
But just big enough
For the nail scissors.

For Ted and Leonard

The bird was broken.
Cracked open. Split like a pod.
From inside its Siamese halves
Its two fathers looked up
At the sky they had made,
And the creatures that had crawled
Out of the pit of each
Sibling mind and lived,
Breathing, with heartbeat,
Even as their own failed.

Each pulsed like a lung
In his half-shell,
Blowing the beak like a horn
To make it speak; their shared mouth.
Until one ceased. The other, listened
In disbelief. Waiting, waiting, waiting
For the next word, using his one claw
To draw, mostly himself, as if
The dead half would suddenly
Return to write the narrative,
With stickled fingers pushed into
The other bird-claw glove, pen-held
And laughing at his joke. Instead,
In silence, nothing happened.

The half-bird, still attached
To his memory of being whole,
Found it harder and harder
To think about anything
Except finding his lost part.

So at last, he left
To go looking.

Crow rocked in the dirt, in the wind,
Blameless at last.

The Last Secret

Is the elephant in the room.
We can't speak about it, even though
It stalks you. Thorny-haired,
Its eyes of nostril turning always to you,
As if you have some special smell.

It stalks us next, but for now
It wants you first.
You don't want its word
Anywhere, or in our mouths.
Its presence makes us dumb.

So, it is the elephant in the room.
In my sleep, I take a gun
And shoot it dead. But in the morning
Its weight is at our feet again,
Wanting to be fed.

Its body is on the hearthrug
More faithful than any dog,
And beside the table, and
Beside you in the car, even though
I sit there; its mournful, stupid eyes

Unable to avoid you. Slowly,
Its breath is stealing your breath,
Its heavy feet rest upon
The altar of your chest. Tonight
I am going to kill it again.

Conversation with Death

Death has come to have a look
At his work.
Sitting by my father's coffin, fingers
Linked in his lap like any doctor,
He is smiling.

"You took him too soon,"
I say.

"It wasn't easy," he tells me. "Every time
I found a way to get him,
He slipped out of it.
That first time, I was sure
The cells I chose would do it.
I watered each blessed seed.
I visited daily. My flowers flowered,
But I found he could uproot them
With almost a thought. Each day
Was stolen from me. Even when
I had him by the heart,
Tried to stop it beating,
Held it fast with my two hands, it was as if
He climbed inside his own crawl space
And picked off my fingers, one by one.

"You could have left him longer,"
I protested.

Death frowned. "To take some
Poor soul, car-crashed by the roadside,
Or with bullet holes and

A leg blown off, is easy.
There is no grace in that.

"But to take a Greatness, who fights
With all that accumulated excellence,
Derived from a full time, even
Had in a short time,
Is an art.

"I could have had him in his thirties,
I wanted him then.
I have wanted him all along.
If I told you I nearly
Lifted him off a train when he
Was only forty-two or forty-three, and a
Little arrhythmia was going to be
My percussion's end
To his ebb and flow of corpuscles,
Could you not see
How lucky you are
To have had him for longer?

"I let him ripen on his tree
Like a heavy fruit. But to wait
Until his stalk broke, in his eighties
Or maybe even his nineties, to have him
Roll into my lap like a ripe fig,
Would have ruined me.

"To take him at the peak of his
Perfection, when he was at his
Escaping most cleverest, meant
I really got to achieve something."

Notes

The poems in the two collections that comprise this book cover a twelve-year period. There are several Australian references in *Stonepicker* because I was still living half my time in Western Australia during the writing of many of the poems. Although not essential, I thought a few notes might be useful, especially regarding the British murderers mentioned.

"Stonepicker" (p. 3): A woman who believes she can do no wrong, only that wrong is done to her; she casts blame on others but will not recognize it in herself, and so takes no responsibility for what happens to her.

"Playground" (pp. 4–5): This actually happened at the school I briefly attended in Yorkshire.

"Sisyphus" (p. 13): Sisyphus is a seed poem for my collection *Waxworks*. He is also my father.

"Fear" (p. 14): The night before surgery I was all alone in a Western Australian country hospital feeling scared.

"Dr Shipman" (p. 15): A British doctor who is thought to have killed in excess of 250 people. He was brought to trial in October 1999, began fifteen concurrent life sentences in January 2000, and hanged himself on January 13, 2004.

When people couldn't understand why he wouldn't tell them what motivated him, it seemed most likely that the power of withholding what others wanted was the reason. In this way he retained power right up to and beyond his own death.

"Myra Painting" (p. 32): This is about a painting of Myra Hindley (who died in November 2002) made out of the colored handprints of small children. When exhibited in public, it caused an outcry because Hindley had aided and abetted her lover, Ian Brady, in abusing and murdering several children in the 1960s. Ink was thrown at the painting, which was taken away to be restored. But when I saw the space where it had been at the Sensation exhibition at the Royal Academy in London in 1997, it seemed to me that the remaining ink splodges were all part of the artistic process.

"The Dying Room" (p. 39): Written after watching a documentary on the treatment of unwanted girls in China, and having spoken to childless friends who have since adopted unwanted Chinese girls.

"The Lady M" (p. 46): Drug-taker.

"Laugh" (p. 50): Ridicule and bitching at a party when one of the guests falls over, having drunk too much.

"The San Francisco Fire" (p. 53): On October 20, 1991, I was at the Candlestick stadium in San Francisco with friends when the East Bay fires took hold.

"The Signature" (p. 65): Shortly before he died in October 1998 my father divided up my mother's books between my brother and me. He opened each book to see if she'd signed it, as she usually did. In one book he found the cut-out corner of the page where her signature had been. It was an act of betrayal by a friend, because only someone who came to the house and spent time there as a guest would have known their way around well enough to find the book and cut my mother's signature out.

"For Ted and Leonard" (pp. 66–67): In 2000, two years after my father died, his good friend and illustrative collaborator, Leonard Baskin, also died. My father's most famous creation was *Crow,* and Leonard was famous for his illustrations of my father's bird poems (among other things), so I think of their friendship in terms of the birds they created.

"The Last Secret" (p. 68): Written a month before my father died, this poem explains how I felt about having to keep the secret that he was dying of cancer.

The Book of Mirrors

For Olwyn and in memory of my mother

The Book of Mirrors

The book of mirrors is waiting for faces to fill it;
Polished chrome or pools of mercury
Are not so demanding. Each page
A flat conduit for whatever images
Are directed into it, sending them back
To the glassy eye of the beholder; a mirror
Communicating objects and people
To another mirror. Stripped of artifice or disguise
It gives us back to ourselves
As we really are; it does not recognize
The means by which we layer ourselves
In all manner of fakery.

The book of mirrors does not hold prisoners,
Although it may expose the cage
Of our own constructions.
If we are ready
It may illuminate the door over our left shoulder
Through which we can escape,
Leaving our old skins behind
For others to trip over.

The book of mirrors is always found by the roadside,
Or on a coffee table in a hospital waiting room,
Or on bookshelves belonging to someone
Who has recently died. It is
Upholstered in brown suede
— As if softened calf skin
Could lessen the possibility
Of being made to bleed by a careless grasp.

The book of mirrors is also a book of memories,
It plays us back to ourselves
So that if we care to look
We can see ourselves as others did.
But it does not make judgments
As others might.

The book of mirrors does not reflect
What is artificial or illusory.
If it shows us no reflection at all
Then our disguise is so complete
That whatever we once were
Is lost, and cannot be brought back.
And the book of mirrors does not care.

Stonepicker and the Book of Mirrors

Stonepicker has been collecting wounds as pebbles,
Stopping often to study a stone in the road
For the slight it might have
Inadvertently subjected her to. Taking
No offense where none is meant
Would devoid her of purpose,
So she must find some insult in it.

And there it is, the book of mirrors,
Lying on the verge and begging,
Just begging to be opened
But only because it is shut.
With enquiring fingers
She lifts the brown suede cover
To discover why it was left behind;
And there she is, naked on all of the pages,
Stripped of her guises, false and otherwise,
As if she were Dorian Gray
Degenerating on glass, not canvas.

If she would only
Lay down her sack of grievances
And release her stubborn back
From the burden of habit and the dutiful
Gathering of spite and bile as missiles,
The book might redefine her
As someone else entirely.

January

Hades beckons. The River Styx
Has already eaten parts of the road
And whole cars, before receding to digest
Other swept-away organisms that remain
Trapped in the eddies of its belly.
Some of us are left withering at the water's edge
For other reasons, as the bitter cold
Takes a few of the old before spring;
Leaves the rest of us aging in our grays and blacks
Beneath the skies of gray and black.
Then the gales come. Windy fingers
Working away at window-edges, trees
Giving up their wish to be vertical,
Crashing into hedges that teem
With quivering wildlife.
Snowdrops confound in their masses,
Gathering as if for chapel in their bright whites
With green cuffs. And somewhere at night
A dog barks endlessly, as if
To keep the winter devils away
But unable to guard anything more
Than the one spot he stands on.

Stunckle's Night Out

See him walk.
Hear him talk.
Watch him pour alcohol
Into a man whose woman
He would have. Not laughing,
Just pouring. He would not leave
The poor drunk be.

See him eat, his eyes
Upon the young girl's breasts;
His food escapes his lips
As he stares sideways
At that younger chest.

He feigns an interest in the partnership
Of his unwitting friends;
He'll separate them if he can
With pincers and a tweezer-grip.

The Sign

*(The flax root was found in January 2008 in Japan
and became a local attraction.)*

A man in Japan notices a flax root on a stall
In the shape of a naked man and woman.
He pays a heavy price for his recognition ($60),
And takes the couple home.
Now his home becomes an attraction.
Everyone wants to see what nature threw up
Out of her own belly. They arrive in buses
To witness the marvel — and each other:
People watching people watching a vegetable
In the shape of people.
They think it's a sign, although of what
Remains to be determined.
They believe it to be magic or a miracle;
It gives them hope. Hope hangs
Outside the man's house in the shape of people,
And imbued with credibility by other people.
This engenders jealousy in some quarters,
So, one night, when the crowds have gone home
Or retired to their tents to sleep,
Someone cuts down the misshapen root
And boils it up for herb tea.
The conjoined couple bubble until
They are nothing more than an impotent brew;
Hope as vegetable stew.

Self-examination

I pace the house,
I draw the bath,
I pour the tea, I pretend
A note to myself will become
The poetry of myself;
I prevaricate incessantly.

I follow myself around,
And if I turn, agitated at the sound
Of those other footsteps
I come right up face to face
With myself, both of us
Astonished to be here.

The Cure

Take these pills, two a day,
And that loose coil
That tangles in your skull
Calling itself a mental process
Or even a brain
Will tighten right up.
You'll not want to stick your fingers
Down your throat again.

I sat, skinny at seventeen but
Feeling the rolls of flesh
Weigh heavily on my bones;
A plate of liver and onions took on a chill
As I negotiated its dietary properties.
Nothing fattening in that
Says the cook, passing over two pills,
Which I pocketed in my cheek
Wedged up against my teeth
And spat down the toilet.
No mood-altering medication
Would ever take me
For ransom or otherwise.
Give me the raw materials; the black holes,
The cold floors and confusion of needles-as-thoughts
That make me feel myself,
Over any stupefying potions
That would turn me into someone else.

Dead Starling

Held in the starling's beak
Like small, white pearls in a ghastly
Rotting crevice
Was a perfect clutch of fly eggs.

In hours, maggots would break out
To eat the brain.
I am puzzled by the bird's expression;
One eye is closed as if sleeping,
But the other is awake,
Turning and turning in the socket
Behind the delicate white thread
That lines the edge of the cavity: A fly
Has found itself hatched in the hollow.
It revolves like an ebony iris,
Searching for a door to the cranium
That is not there; it has outgrown
All the exits. Its black thorax
Glistens at me sightlessly.

Anticipating Stones

I've paced the flat earth;
I've shorn the green wilderness
The shortest it's ever been;
I've dug in trees like full stops
And bushes like semi-colons;
I've imagined where walkways and avenues
Will begin. I've dug so not to block
A path to anywhere
And there, in my mind,
As heavy and round and cool
As if they were real
Are the stones.
My boulders bloom
Like white orb mushrooms,
Big as fallen moons.
They're almost here. Anticipation
Rivets me at night, I'm fastened
To the mattress in my sleep,
Digging holes to place them in; upended,
Statuesque, earth's offspring as sculpture
Beside the pond I've traced with paint
Beneath the cedar tree.

Part-timer

He is fourteen, gardening.
He sits at the kitchen table without syllables;
The expulsion of air
That indicates "yes" or "no"
Is almost inaudible,
So he must repeat himself.
His shy spring coils inside him,
Readying a more unguarded sound
That may stun him
So I might hear.
It's a step at a time to know him,
And his favorite labels for shirts,
And shoes and jackets. They are
The vocabulary he uses to define himself.
I smile.
He smiles;
He's learned that. The first time
I praised him he stared back
As if not understanding;
He knows a job badly done
Will be commented on,
But this new sound
Is one that drives him on.

Woman Falling

The car has been driven off the cliff.
She sits there, in the driver's seat,
Watching the scenery as the rocks on the left
Give way to trees. The crimson horizon
Turns pink and swings upwards
As the surface of the earth,
Divided by water and carbuncled
By granite outcrops, speeds to meet her.
Over and over again she recalls
The instant that her foot slipped from the brake
To accelerate, in a moment of uncertain conviction
To do, or not to do, something
That might have consequences.
She was egged on, it was true,
"Make your mark!" they cried
From the far side of the ravine,
"Reach for the sky!" But, like Icarus,
When his wax and feathers met the hot sun
Beyond the walls of his prison
And he fell to earth,
Her metal machine cannot fly.
And here she is, falling
And waiting
And falling.

Stunckle Goes to a Party

Stunckle readjusts his balls
Beneath his lightweight trousers;
He is going to a party
Where he expects to see
Many pretty girls.
He tucks his formal red shirt
Into his waistband
And hopes they will know he means business.
Oh, when the music plays
See how he barely smiles,
Oh, when the girl gazes up at him,
Dazed, in some kind of adoration
(Or confusion)
See how he just ducks an eye
In her direction.
He touches her shoulder and something
Beneath her skin flinches. He thinks
It must be the power of his personality
Burning through the tips of his fingers
Like an electrical charge.
The girl shudders a little, her smile falters.
Something is wrong.

Statue 1

See me here, on my plinth,
Oddly angular, bitten away in parts;
Peculiarly shaped. Eroded.
There was a woman once —
Didn't like me. Dead now.
She'd walk past me, eyes averted,
Ignoring my greetings
In the hallway of my own home,
A visitor, not related to me.
Chip, chip, the bits would flake
From the raw material that I was.

See how she made my club foot,
And how each painful encounter
Allowed by others
Who'd not sully her externals
By admitting her predisposition
To little cruelties
Has made me a limb as a weapon.

Spoon

You dropped the spoon.
She detected its fall;
Picked out the metal that made it,
Sensed the weight of its body
As it incised a path through the air,
So knew how slow it tipped and spun.

She measured the time between
The handle as it hit the wooden floor
And the bowl, resonating a different pitch
Like a second voice.

All this from a moment that escaped you.
Her blindness collected it,
An eye in each fingertip,
For you, who see,
And lost it.

Preparing the Ground

Like the portent of doom,
My grandmother flies in from the north.
The magnetic pole of her presence
Appears to repel my father.
He goes away for a couple of days,
And my grandmother splits open
Her face at her smile
As if taking each side of her mouth
In her two hands
And pulling it apart,
To allow her doppelgänger to scramble
From the lip-noose of opened granny-bag
And step into the hallway.

I watch the flare of her nostrils; the caverns
In which her wind blasts,
As she leads me to the garden
To watch over my six-month-old brother.
Eyeing the boy,
Bottom-anchored by his diaper,
I reckoned it would be two days
Before he crawled as far as the undergrowth
Into which he might disappear.
Convinced of his immobility
I follow my grandmother's scent
Back into the dark burrow
Of the central hallway.
She is raging,
Her storm has been
My mother's marriage long in the brewing.
"You must leave him!" she cries;
This new woman has no warmth

For her son-in-law.
"He'll be seeing 'her' you know,
The wastrel, the faithless scoundrel."

Making a cake, my mother
Scrapes the mixture into a baking tin,
But her tears overcome her
And the kitchen's too small to weep in,
So she sits at the larder table
Unable to contain her wretchedness.

"You must come home with me,"
Says my grandmother, elated,
As if she has won something.
If my father only knew
How she became someone
He'd not met before
When he wasn't looking
He'd never have walked out that door;
He'd carry us away to safety
And not look back at the unloose witch
And her coven of one,
Her spite and her bile
Gut-rotting her into
A stomach-stapling.

My mother holds her face
In the bucket of her hands,
She doesn't notice my grandmother's smile
As she picks up the forgotten sponge
And places it exactly
In the center of the oven.

Seeing me brotherless
My grandmother brings him in
From the garden.
I have already considered
Placing him near in the hope he can hear,
So that when he speaks at last
He'll bear witness to all that has passed.
But now I see he is dumber than it will take
To ever remember.

My mother beds him down
In the cot in my bedroom corner,
Her own, chipping away at her
As if she were an egg,
To be broken and beaten
And turned into something else.
My grandmother stills her beak
From pitting holes
In the ground of my mother's skull
Into which she pours salt
When she sees me watching,
Not missing a thing; eavesdropping.

She picks me up
And carries me to her bed
In the room my father writes in,
The sheets are as cold as glass
On my bare legs. I'm hugging
My frozen knees in my nightdress,
Wishing, wishing to be saved
From the magic carpet
Of my grandmother's prayer.

"Would you like to come live with me?"
She says, and I ball all my questions
Up into my incapable mouth.
My tongue is helpless, but to ask;
"Can Daddy come?" Meaning everything.
"We'll see," she replies,
Her face as hard as pyrite.
I know as she leaves the room
That I am losing my father.

I can hear my grandmother's voice
Like a machine
Grinding at my mother some more
As I creep past my bedroom door. Downstairs,
I stand at the black Bakelite telephone.
Someone must tell my father
Before his children are taken.
I gaze at the pages of notebooks
All covered in scrawl, and realize
That I cannot read.

Even if I knew where to find him,
When I place my finger in the dial
And pull, it barely moves,
My finger buckles, useless at the knuckle.
My grandmother's engine
Is the background hum
On the drum of my ear.
My father is too far away to hear
His mother-in-law's tongue
Flaying.

Puberty

There's no disguising them, they're huge,
Buttressed on my rib cage like
Two melon-ends, when all my friends
Are sticks without a shape. They're gorgeous
In bikinis on the beaches,
And gape at me in T-shirts
That stretch across my reaches.
I cannot hide them in a sack
Of shirts that flap like sails,
When the fabric hangs so tent-like
I look as though I house
A pair of nursing whales.
My arms are always folded
As if to hide my front,
But my thighs are beams that hold aloft
The building I've become
And nothing could be large enough
To camouflage my rump.

Stunckle Sings

My life's afloat.
I'm sailing on a gentle breeze, an airborne boat,
My coat is flapping at my knees,
Achilles has nothing on me.

I see compassion, distant once,
A sometimes enemy,
Being kind enough to keep at bay
The barbs and arrows thrown your way.

It's easier to let me speak
To those you wish were gone,
My intellect a sharper spike
Than yours, to hang a head on.

I can rise above the heads
Of those who'd hold me accountable,
When righteousness is by my side
My truth is insurmountable.

God and I are siblings,
Our secrets be the glue,
We know the truth,
We know the truth,
It's not for you.

Flea

I finally murdered
The unrecognizable scrap of black matter
That now lacks shape, or spring, and dangles
Its threads of legs helplessly; this dead thing
Has left my ankles raw, my flesh
Sore and itching, blisters festering
As my blood boils beneath infected skin
And zinc bandages, weeping.
This shapeless pinhead that's barely visible,
This polished coal from a hobbit's fire,
This bundle of poisonous jaw
And thorax of ire, this torturer's apprentice
With his infected needles,
This burrowing bloodsucker
With his spring-loaded leap that ate my feet
And chewed a necklace of holes in the meat
Of my leg-ends; this thrower of parties
For his parasitic little friends
Is a dead end.

Fingers

His fingers' thought rose
From the hand that slept.
It met the woman's idea
Of her skin, as her eyes
Travelled the width of her closed lids,
Seeing inwards.

The moment of contact
Felt by the nerve endings
In the landscape of her body,
At the point where hip met thigh,
Connected her to the thought
Of the man's fingers.

Attached to the thought
Came the sleeping hand,
Attached to the hand,
Now a palm's slow progress
Across the fields, was an arm.
Attached to the arm, curious
At the journey taken,
The body of a man,
Waking.

My Mother

They are killing her again.
She said she did it
One year in every ten,
But they do it annually, or weekly,
Some even do it daily,
Carrying her death around in their heads
And practicing it. She saves them
The trouble of their own;
They can die through her
Without ever making
The decision. My buried mother
Is up-dug for repeat performances.

Now they want to make a film
For anyone lacking the ability
To imagine the body, head in oven,
Orphaning children. Then
It can be rewound
So they can watch her die
Right from the beginning again.

The peanut eaters, entertained
At my mother's death, will go home,
Each carrying their memory of her,
Lifeless — a souvenir.
Maybe they'll buy the video.

Watching someone on TV
Means all they have to do
Is press "pause"
If they want to boil a kettle,

While my mother holds her breath on screen
To finish dying after tea.

The filmmakers have collected
The body parts,
They want me to see.
They require dressings to cover the joins
And disguise the prosthetics
In their remake of my mother;
They want to use her poetry
As stitching and sutures
To give it credibility.
They think I should love it —
Having her back again, they think
I should give them my mother's words
To fill the mouth of their monster,
Their Sylvia Suicide Doll,
Who will walk and talk
And die at will,
And die, and die
And forever be dying.

Painter

It's his dance.
He writes the music. He takes
His belly-crawl and adolescent stumble,
His last laugh and his marriages,
His son and his years alive,
And grinds them to powder
For his reds, blues and grays.
With his brush he makes each stroke
Sound on canvas taut as pregnant skin;
A perfect note. He gives
Each begging mute he paints
Its voice, he plucks their harp,
Each shape a rhythmic quote;
His thought-provoking symphonies
In every work of art.

Harpist

The gilt wing rests upon his shoulder.
The strings that are each feather-shaft,
Stripped down to their core
To reveal the sinew
Of each musical note,
Divide the world of his left
From his right.
And in the silence of that split
He brings his two spiders to meet
At the fingertips.
They glance at one another,
They reach out to touch,
But don't, and flirt.
Coquettish, their knees glitter as they dance,
Each against the other's underside.
Each movement and stride
Strikes a consonant or vowel
In the syllables of their dialogue.
Their dance is mutual persuasion,
The sublimation of their conversation,
And they are so in love.

Message to a Habitual Martyr

You blame me
For all that's wrong with your life
And the ills that beset you,
But you did things too.

I'd no idea that I was an obstacle,
A stone in your ground
Which would distract your direction
Or unravel your purpose.

I was ignorant that you credited me
With so much importance
That you couldn't step over
Or walk around.

There are things I could blame you for too;
If I tried, I could hate you,
But what good would it do
To be so tormented?

I know that they were then
And this is now, instead I'll wish
For a small kindness in the future
That would obliterate them anyhow.

I'll step over them, all the steeper
For their accumulated pointlessness,
Because in the face of death
They are meaningless.

There's love here too,
Overcoming who did what to whom,

It's past and gone
And unimportant now, who won,

Since retribution is a tool
Employed by such a fool
As wants to pay back what is done,
Instead of moving on.

And here we walk,
Our shadows long, our years diminishing,
Our chances pass and when they're gone
There's nothing, nothing, nothing.

The Letter

The unopened letter lies upside down
Beneath a Screwfix catalogue and two bank statements;
It has hooks in it. My first glance at the envelope
Brought me no joy. I think it may be
A punitive thing requiring compliance.
Manipulating.
So if I leave it there, properly unread,
Perhaps time will alleviate it
Of its importance — or lack of it.
Perhaps time will rot the paper down
Beneath listings for power drills and band saws.
Perhaps it is a figment of my imagination
And I only had the idea of a letter
Being delivered and signed for.
If I don't look at it long enough
Perhaps it will go away.

The Head

Yesterday they took a head
And filmed it for TV.
It was sliced right off
By an irate Iraqi
With a mask and sword.
He waited for the blindfolded American
To identify himself,
Then bisected the man's jugular,
Separating chin from chest,
Brain from beating heart.

Wars will end, they said,
And be as over and dead
As the soldiers. What news then?
What point, the poetry?
But here it is again, war
With a severed head.

Stunckle and the Book of Mirrors

Stonepicker's uncle has heard about a magic book
That will give him all the answers,
And show him the door he needs
To move on to the next stage in his life.

He thinks he is ready.
He has polished his cranium until it shines,
Even from the inside so that everything
That passes through its machinery
Is analyzed by one of the sharpest brains
In the country. His desire, now,
Is to be applauded in the pages
Of a book that will have recorded
Just for him, his excellence, his achievements,
And the sheer number of his many talents.

He is sitting with a wounded digit
(Having shut it in a car door)
In a doctor's waiting-room, when he notices
A brown suede book resembling
An over-size bible. The edge, not golden
But glassy, gleams with eager promise
At shiny openings. He lifts the cover
And there is the ceiling of the room,
And there are the walls, there are also versions
Of the other patients, uglied or airbrushed
By the all-seeing honesty
Of the pages. Stunckle tilts the book
Towards his face, braced
For whatever it exposes of him.
He believes that he may see a saint;

That the book will validate him
And he can hardly wait.

He peers into the glass — but it is empty of his features.
Panic rising, he knows in his stony heart
That there is no way he has ceased to exist —
He has to be in there somewhere.
He tilts the book down at his chair to see
If any part of him is mirrored,
But there is only a section of rectum
On the spot where he ought to be.

Love Poem to a Down's Syndrome Suicide Bomber

On February 1, 2008, Al-Qaeda blew up
two Down's syndrome women in Baghdad pet markets.

Oh, you are so beautiful. I think I love you.
I see how your skin glows
With the innocence born of your disability,
But that does not trouble me.
You are so fresh and new and pure; I would not sully
Such authenticity as yours.
Please, do not grow cold; wear this padded waistcoat
Beneath your clothes; a gift from me.
In our hours apart it will be
The promise of my embrace. I long
To be with you again. Your radiance,
Your light, and all your separate pieces
Will illuminate my night.

No, I cannot follow you.
My sacrifice is to remain behind,
Have children and another life,
Knowing I have rid our world
Of your affront in being
And others of your kind.

Doppelgänger

The girl who would be me
Keeps fifty photos of my dead father
On the walls of her living-room.
Motherhood is a badge she wears
When she produces children to accommodate
The need for heirs, as I have none.

She likes my father
Better than her own, for reasons known
Only to herself; he'll not remarry to alleviate
His loneliness, replacing her dead mother
With someone other than a woman
To whom she can relate.

The Problem

Your consideration gives it shape.
Where there was nothing before,
You have reached into the void
And pulled it up, up, out of the black
And into the sunlight
In order to see it more clearly.

Your comparison of it to the other
Thoughts that occupy your head
Gives it size. It is enormous;
A nagging lump that overshadows
All the easier tasks and undertakings
With its huge importance.

Being large gives it weight,
And, because it is yours, expanding
To preoccupy your every deliberation,
You find your shoulders buckling
Beneath the bulk of it, your head
So clogged your neck might snap.

Now your problem has shape, size and weight,
You can properly identify it.
You decide it is a mountain,
Unconquerable by joy, or will, or effort.
You give up and lie down in its shadow
To wait for the carrion eaters to come.

As you lie there, in the same dark
From which the problem first emerged,
It occurs to you that its very nature
Defines it as owning a solution.

If there is none, then it is not a problem,
It is an insurmountable obstacle.

The insurmountable obstacle towers over you.
In fact, it appears to have grown.
You beg it to go away, but being insurmountable
It doesn't move. Instead,
It grows roots and harbors small mammals
Beneath its rocky outcrops.

The insurmountable obstacle has fed
On your veneration of its significance,
And become productive. If ignored,
It will develop a climate.
You ask yourself what to do,
Faced with the permanence of this obstruction.

Uselessly falling down before it
Has left its evolution unaffected.
Better to face it, size it up,
Take its measure and visualize its edges.
Then, imagining yourself at a point beyond it,
Walk around it.

At Fourteen

I have never been so hated.
I loathe myself, my flesh
As firm and proud beneath my fingers
As any pig's, encasing bones in layers
Of apple pie encrusted
With last month's custard,
And the second helpings
Of all the fish au gratins
That I believed I'd run off later.
America comes and goes
Like a handbag, with an uncle
And two cousins in it,
And a grandmother singing
Her sacrifices like Hail Marys,
As if she will absolve herself
By repetition. But I'm still
Pressure-cooking beneath the tight surface
Of my overstretched skin,
Unable to escape myself
No matter which country I'm in.

Like Sisters

Think of two poles,
Two Norths or Souths
Repelling one another through
Their identical magnetic reflections.
That's her and me. Alike,
Stalagmite attached to stalactite,
Each misinterpreting the other
In whose head we are reversed.

Two Women

Two women sit in different houses
At four o'clock in the morning
In different parts of the country
Joined by an umbilical rope,
That first one tried to cut,
Then the other tried to cut,
That just kept knitting up
And passing poison between them;
It is a magic umbilical cord,
It is the idea of an umbilical cord,
Really, it is love unrequited, experienced
Always by one at the very moment
The other is driven away
By some means perceived
But not necessarily, honestly, real.
Each woman wants the other
To see her reason, her purpose,
And that she is absolutely
Inarguably right.

One of the women rises from her chair
Collects the milk from the doorstep
And ceases to care
About being right.
She turns out the light
And walks upstairs.
The umbilical rope that she shared
Curls and twists uselessly behind her
In the dark of the hallway,
Like a headless snake.
The other woman

Is still tied to its tail,
Being right the way mothers
Are always right.

About a Poem

There's a poet in there somewhere.
Did you skim over the words
Expecting the message to leap out and grab you?
You'll miss him. He'll be
Tucked under the iambic pentameter,
It's five feet cornering
The poet's meaning.

Don't expect him all laid out
Like a diagram with arrows pointing,
He might have hidden himself in allegory.
Read him twice, aloud.
Hear the way he speaks, be judicial
Instead of searching for the easy way out
And skimming, interested
Only in the superficial
One-note shout.

Stunckle's Cousin

I will not review your conceits.
You are safe enough in your efforts,
Attached as they are to your ego.
I will not even mention your name
Lest your vanity polish and blind us.

You snap the new growth and skin the bark
Of other trees for your bonfire,
But when the ashes cool,
What will you have made?
You break things.
You stand on the fallen trunks
Of those you talk about;
Could you not see over the wall on your own?
Too short, I guess.

You believe you have immunity
In the right to judge others with impunity
As any Caesar would award himself
Before he burns,
Or falls on the knife
Of those closest. Your shadow
Long ago left your side,
Your pride being disproportionate
To your abilities; it could no longer
Justify its attachment.

Breaking down what others construct
Means you inhabit the debris.
When you're buried in rubble
Right up to your stubble
We'll bring on the flesh-eating ants,
Sell tickets and dance.

Gift-Horses

Should never be closely examined,
Since a found flaw will impair
The immediate, appropriate, joyful response.
Their teeth are sure to be either absent
Or sharpened and fastened on
To some part of your anatomy,
To be noticed the moment
The giver is gone.
Sometimes we must accept the toothless
Or the sharp-jawed,
Although we instinctively know
That our gift-horse is flawed,
Or comes with conditions
Buried in its hide like blowflies.
Who knows what a ride
The creature will give us
If taken in? Be pleased to keep it,
And should it fall to the floor
Beneath the weight of its responsibility
To be something useful and free,
Recycle and eat it.

Stunckle's Wish for a Family

He cannot wear his sister's dress
Too tight across the chest, he cannot
Marry her history and mother
The orphans he'd smother.
He's a backward cuckoo,
Not in the nest, but outside,
All around it like Red Indians.

To the Victor, an Empty Chalice

See their gritted teeth and glassy stare
Fixated on whatever it is
They want to get hold of.
Glittering or shining,
Or promising supreme satisfaction,
It is going to cost them more
In time, or effort, or money,
Than they will ever win.
It could be a man or a woman,
Or their own way, or the conclusion
Of a well-thought-out plan.
Their perpetual state is confrontation.
Their lawyer's on speed-dial to secure
The secrecy of their efforts;
The corpse of their smile
Reflects all the little deaths
Behind their ocular pebbles,
That record their success. Whatever it is,
Hand it over. Look,
They want it so badly.
Their whole life is the fight, it defines them,
Without it, they're pointless.
Let them win and fall over
Or continue to suffer their malice.
Let them have it tonight, just give in.
Be free from conflict
And allow them the prize:
To the victor, an empty chalice.

Here We Begin

We are forged
In our mother's womb
Where our voice is given in two parts;
Our means of expression
And making ourselves understood
Is always our parents' echo
In the ears of the intransigent.

How to Kill a Scorpion

When the queen-size bed is lifted
From the floor of your Australian home
And carried off to furnish two other bodies
With its vociferous springs
And optimistic suspension,
Do not tread on the brown leaf
That lies crisply beneath it.
Examine it for legs, and see there are eight,
With pincers, and a tail that arcs
In a reflex over the segmented thorax
To dangle the lamp of its poison,
Ready for anything. Cajole it
Into a plastic container
That may once have held margarine,
Replace the lid, melt holes in the top
With hot match heads,
And wonder what scorpions eat.
Then forget it for as long as it takes
For all your possessions to be sea-freighted
Back to England.

Three years later, when the box stacks
Of bed-linen, lamp bases and book shelves
Are released from storage
And delivered in the back of a pantechnicon,
Open the margarine container and say,
"Oh, that's what happened to the scorpion!"
Put it in a glass display case
With fossils and shells and be glad
That it never found your foot at the bedside,
Or made your slippers a place to hide.

Stunckle as Eyeglass

Honor is not satisfied.
Justice is not done.
Promises remain broken.

This man stands before all comers.
He is the cornea through which
He would have you look and see
His probity. His good is magnified;
His less redeeming qualities
Made small as blisters
In the concave of his glassy arc
Where truth is stupefied.

And from his righteous side
Your ills are magnified,
Your good lost in re-editing
Through the poison window of
His optic skin.

Ended

So was that it?
Snapped coral stick of glass
Its broken leg and bone stuck out,
All wet with wine.

There we poured;
Our liquid spilt
And soaking in. Our faces visible
Only as long as wet reflected us.

Was that our time?
It was as bright
As any light that cost plenty,
And in that flash
I am still blinded,
Unable to see
The reason for your fury.

Jesus in Brugge

I.

Jesus sits before me,
Life-size on a table,
And I am the audience; one person
In a clutch of wooden chairs.
People pass respectfully,
Eyes averted from me.
But I am not praying,
I am studying the intricacy of Jesus;
His right hand raised,
His two fingers blessing all comers,
And listening to the hundreds of years
Of hope and prayer that cling
To every crease of his clothing,
Every curling wooden tendril of his hair.

II.

Thousands have touched
The right knee of Jesus
As they walked by — and his bare feet.
The grain of the wood from which he is made
Is polished by years of human oil
And the soft buffing of wishes and skin.
I can hear the cacophony
That resides in the folds of his wooden gown;
Where prayers like hoards of insects
Seek refuge.

Stunckle's Truth

He'll take your words and make a noose
To hang you from the garden spruce,
He'll change your truth to something else
In order to defend himself.

Black is white and white is black,
He'll beat you with it till you crack,
Lies are truth and truth can lie,
Stones can swim and camels fly.

For Margot

December 25, 2005

Yesterday you died.
But still I think of you
As brightly lit
As any stained glass window,
Slim as a willow
In your dress of many colors
Against its background of black,
Your hair in dark cascades
To the nether reaches of your back.
Your sun drew satellites
As such magnetism might, as you became
A flame to those demanding light.

Know that you were greatly loved by us;
The distance of half the planet
Did not diminish that.
In the memories I keep
I hear you speak as clearly now
As that last time I saw you,
When we pulled up a bar stool in Melbourne
To escape the winter rain.
More fragile then, your hair so short;
I feared we'd never meet again.
We toasted health
And drank our last champagne.

The Idea of a Dog

The idea of a Rottweiler grew legs
And walked. Its big, square head
Atop the solid, barreled torso
Looked up, waiting for instruction
Or embrace. The idea was obedient,
Faithful, intimidating to others,
But the idea was lopsided.
So the idea developed a twin brother.
Now, in my head, I'd say "sit"
And they would, dogs in duplicate,
Each reflecting the other identically.
I could see myself walking the streets
Flanked by muscles moving in tandem
Over the powerful shoulders
Of my synchronized keepers.
Perhaps I'd redden my lips,
Wear sunglasses
And a very short skirt.

Nearly Fifty

Look, I'm escaping!
I'm running out of hours like a clock
On its last circuit; time
Is slipping through the gaps between my fingers
Like beach sand, leaving cockle shells, airline tickets,
Dried curls of seaweed, condoms and old crisp packets
As a reminder that something happened once
In this disappearing life. Even as I stand before you
I'm losing brain cells like marbles. Please do not
Trip over them as you exit.

If I run fast enough I may
Catch up with myself searching
For what happened to myself
When I wasn't looking.
And if I do, what will I say?
Perhaps I'll pull up a chair
And invite myself to sit.
Perhaps I will have accomplished
Those mountains of tasks that drag on strings
Like tin cans tied to a wedding car bumper,
Reminding me of their
Completely unnecessary urgency.
Or perhaps I will simply have cut them free.

Stunckle's Uncle

Onomatopoeia rules the scablands
Where his inner landscape
Is the stuff of sweaty nightmares.
He must walk it daily even as his feet
Trace the earth's crust in actuality.
He is one country inside another,
He is possessed of contrast; when trees
Rise above his filthy head in which
No thoughts (of love or compassion) can breathe,
Internally his desert hisses and spits its envy.
He knows he's somehow failed; his years
Are hanging heavy at his wattle now,
Like necklace parasites. But still he cannot see
That lack of small humanity
Has kept him plastic with intent
To foster ignorance.

Thin Woman in Search of Perfection

Slim as a toothpick she barely
Got away with wearing that perfect little black
"Sex dress" beneath which
Her legs spidered in black stockings,
Knees like carbuncles, feet
Like tapered palette knives bound up
In the black and metal straps of French heels.

Her shoulders were a bow,
The unstrung arrow had already
Made a hole in her somewhere;
She was leaking out a little at a time,
Imperceptibly. She was too pale
Against the bottle-black pudding-bowl haircut
That cradled her continually surprised expression.
Her bloodless skin from the back of a cave
Never wore rouge, but she
Encircled her pale eyes in kohl
Like a gothic doll, no color
In the bloom of those irises, only her lips
Were scarlet. An opening of flesh
Like a red slice in white paper;
She was drawing herself in
With ink and scissors, perfectly,
Not ever coloring outside the lines.

Obsessed, she made perfect cocktails
From a book. Wiped each drip between pourings
Until I longed to shout
"Leave it until last!" The perfect dinner for which
I had avoided lunch as its enormous proportions
Preceded it by description,

Was a light salad. Caesar had beaten me to it,
And eaten half of it by the time it reached me.
But the sauce was perfect. It was only as I waited
For the main course that I realized
The evening was already over; a perfect coffee
Was placed by my hypoglycemic elbow.

Recently, her perfect man had left her,
Which wasn't perfect at all.
She'd phone her ex
For blackmail sex:
"You do not love me, you do not love me,"
She'd cry. And he didn't.
But would find himself attempting to deny
What would save him; her perfect pain
And the news of her projectile vomiting
Was laid at his door daily.
He could only escape if he'd decide
To be the perfect bastard.

She was drying up like a riverbed.
There was nothing that could travel the route
Of her colon. I watched her ulna and radius
Manipulate the thumb that held her wineglass.
"Look how thin I am!" she cried,
Like some proud mother of a clever child.
"He is doing this to me!"

On the night of the party she wore lilac.
The first thing I noticed was her spine;
It was a mountainous worm that slid
Down her back and lumped

Beneath the pale chiffon. Oh, she thought
She was so pretty.

I touched her bare skin, thin and wan
As pale silk, stretching
Over the bone of her shoulder.
If I twisted it a door might open
Or I would snap her clavicle.
The stoop was a half-circle now;
The bow was breaking. She turned
Her party mask to face me.
Above it shone the rising moon of her forehead,
Prominent as a gravestone
Above the holes that contained
The bloodshot balls of her eyes.

She smiled; her lips were gone, lipstick
All introverted, her teeth
Arched out at me, they were the bleached scales
Of her skull edge, the gums had left them huge
And fleshless in their departure.

In her perfect dress, a purple bow at the back
Of the marble post of her neck
On which her head balanced precariously,
She danced, the amethyst discs at her earlobes
Gleaming either side of her hollows,
And like everything else
She was perfect at it.

Assia Gutmann

I open a book of Jewish poetry
And there's her maiden name,
Translating as she never
Translated me. A child then,
I couldn't understand
The cross-patch plaster stuck
On her concerned forehead,
As she slept in her airline mask
In the afternoons as if
Youth could be got back again.
I could tell her now,
It's only in dreams
As our skin betrays us.

Her beauty frightened me
Carved as she was of piano keys,
Her hair the black flats,
Her voice on the pedals.

My cloak of invisibility
Was stitched so beautifully,
And she herself made
The black velvet party dress
I begged her to put a white lace collar on,
So I'd look less funereal
Even if Puritan. I'd no idea
How my mother's face reflected
In the polished coals of her eyes
So that she saw right through me,
Not to the inner workings of my mind,
But to the wall behind.

Three Views of a Car Crash

1. Disbelief
If a tree falls and no one sees it,
Is it really still upright?
If a fish leaps a weir
Is it really still swimming in the river below
Because no one witnessed it?
When a car crashes
And only one of three people remains conscious
To be cut out by two firemen
When the others have already been removed,
Does that mean the firemen were illusions?
Were they born only in the mind of the girl
Who could not, in all logic, be otherwise extracted
Without dismemberment of the metal fist
That pinioned her by the breaks in its knuckles?
When the unconscious awoke,
Went off and had other lives, disbelieving
That such a drama ever took place
Because their eyes were not open
To validate the rescue, does this mean
That the girl remains trapped
In the scrapped and buckled metal,
Not rescued at all?

2. Red Cortina
There was an accident when I was
Barely eighteen
And a back-seat passenger in a mini
Hit head-on by a driver, speeding,
His bright red Cortina with sporty spotlights
In checkered covers

Wrong-sided on the road,
Our unbelted bodies hurtling.
He stumbled from his car, dented, lip bleeding,
Leaving the vehicle I was in
Crushed into the hedgerow
Somewhat smaller than it had been.
A bus of lookers came and went
Not even alighting.
At last two firemen hacked off the doors,
For the front passenger whose top half
Rested on the bonnet,
And the woman pinned behind the wheel.
Then they held out their arms for me,
But my legs were trapped beneath
The seat that blocked the door,
Crushed into the concertinaed floor.
They cut away the roof and side
And made a gap just wide enough
To pull me free.

But disbelief in the minds of those
Who had not observed the rescue
Repeats the impact every time I am reminded.
It was as if the accident
Happened yesterday; that other car
Just keeps crashing into me
Because those who still refuse to see
The truth of it, tie me to the memory.

3. Falling Up
I fell through the hole cut in the roof
Of a crashed car, into the arms

Of two firemen with a circular saw
Who cradled me to an ambulance
When my legs dragged like logs.

I fell through my father's
Telephone call to the hospital
Where I lay unregistered
Eight hours in a hallway,
Unable to put two steps together
And reach a telephone.

I fell through the disbelief of others;
The floor came up
And hit me when someone reached out
But not to embrace me.
I was still falling
Long after they'd left the room.

I fell through six months
And one flight of stairs,
Treading splinters. My own nerve-ended pendulums
Spat and scalded against the pathways.
I bypassed the earth's core
And the crust of Australia;
The sky on the other side
Released me into space
As I continued my trajectory.
Now I was not falling;
I was soaring through clouds
With the kookaburras.

The Reason for Not Being

The six-year-old daughter that I never had
Sits on her bed-edge kicking her heels.
I ask what ails her.
"Children," she said. "*Must* we have them?
Look at how many we are already."
— I could see she was feeling her numbers
And they were in the millions.
"If we become more, where will we go?"
"They'll build new houses," I told her.
"But when they run out of space, what then?"
"That's beyond your lifetime," I consoled her.
Although I could see this didn't fix the problem.
"It has to stop," she said, "why can't they admit
That we're like an infestation of locusts
That constantly crave to be fed?
Someone must do something, Mummy please,
Do not give birth to me;
Have a litter of puppies instead."

Poet with Thesaurus

This, said my father, lovingly,
Stroking the beaten-up paperback like a small cat,
Is the book your mother kept beside her
As she wrote those incredible poems.
He held it towards me, a flaming baton
That could illuminate the blank walls
Inside my head. I felt a cheat
To open up the pages and read
New meanings. Shouldn't my mind
Struggle for the words I needed?
Owning each, a solid fruit of labor?
A dictionary will give a word
Its definition and purpose,
So why not use that other book
For the same logical intention?
How limiting such willful blindness is; what fool
Would damn someone who seeks
To use a source of knowledge as a tool?

Things My Father Taught Me

That I was not less than anyone, or a man.
That I could do anything I put my mind to.
But my mind was a sugar-monkey
That harbored enough self-doubt
To bring me to my knees,
So that the only way left was up
And it was up to me.

Firstborn

Born new and bloody,
Unpicked from the placenta and placed
In arms that could never
Hold you long enough.

Looked-for like mail,
You were opened, gaping up
And ready for anything. Your cry,
So short against the walls,

Was finding boundaries
At the arm's length of an echo
In a room for beginners.
The fates sent gifts

And a white ivory elephant.
Hope brought blindness
To what must come.
Better you didn't know,

Though your eyes must have searched
The faces of your mother and father,
Daily, looking, looking.
You must have watched

Those two big people
Pack themselves into that tiny room
Like two foxes, turning and turning to fit,
And you, the pivot in the center of it.

Letters

There's no justice I can do
To the memory of you.
Your letters read as clearly to me now
As they did when written.
Book-bound they might illuminate
The father that you were, so others see
The loss you are to me.

To the Daughter I Never Had

You have been perfect from birth.
You cried only when I was awake
To feed you. You grew rapidly;
One morning you were a squirming,
Teething thing, the next you were three,
Out of nappies, hand on my knee,
Wanting a story at bedtime.
You were all mine; no one else
Contributed a gene to the coloring
Of your eyes, your hair, your skin:
No man left DNA for you to trace the relationship,
Or for me to regret the association
And his predictable absence.
You have loved me unconditionally,
And without the inevitable battle of wills
When reaching puberty. You fulfill your potential.
Your intellectual promise is realized daily;
You waste nothing of yourself
Even in the little things.
You have identified your special skills,
And the man you will marry,
So I can dress in pink silk
With an obscenely large hat,
And drink to your day
Which is made mine by proxy
As I give you away.

To the Daughter I Could Not Be

You didn't love a mother
Who couldn't feel the same
So you did not experience rejection.
You kept silent those questions
That plagued me about adoption and family.
You were charming to guests
But never inquisitive.
You were seen but not heard,
And formed no opinion.
We were both the dishwasher and dryer
But you did not swear you'd never dry
Another plate as soon as leaving home,
While I have kept my word. You did not aspire
To be more than uncomplaining,
Gracious and subservient,
Whereas my character demanded dialogue
In order to better understand,
And give air to what might fester
In another's mind. If dissent
Undid the soft membrane that presented
A fiction outside the four walls we occupied,
I thought it worth the argument.

Your platitudes would irritate my ear
If we were close enough so I could hear.
Your acceptance of demand without question
Demeans you. You are other than I am.
Your compliance makes you the mirror
On the wall of the empty room in which you stand
Between taking dictation or following directions.
Manifesting no reflection of your own

You are the daughter I could not be;
A captive, while I am free.
My root of sibling rivalry.

Jonah and the Whale

You have just seen the launch of the *Titanic*.
The screams of delight,
The hysterical waving,
The tickertape farewell as it slid
Into the ocean like a returning whale.
Your lungs filled with noise,
Your eyes filled with tears,
And back home with your gas cooker
And boiling kettle you knew
You'd seen an event of such importance
That it would saturate you with the memory of it;
But are you changed by it?
After the years have plucked at your skin
Will that towering structure
That rose several stories above you
Still affect you? Will that borrowed moment
Bring a gasp of amazement
From your powdering lips? In fact
If you didn't think much about it
During the passage of time
Time might have taken it back.
But if you'd sailed on the boat
And survived — or died,
Then you and it would be partners;
Either it would have been inside you
Or you would have been inside it.

Crypt

My head is full of graves
Where I have buried my dead,
But in moments of weakness
I hear them calling.

Some of the bodies aren't breathing;
They're friends who are trapped in the moment
When we last spoke before their funeral.
Sometimes I visit the empty spaces
They would occupy if still alive
And lay down the idea of roses in tribute.

Others are the loved and loathsome
Who continue to live and break bread;
It's always the latter who raise their voices in complaint.
The lid of the sarcophagus I nailed down on each one
Is sometimes not heavy enough to prevent an intake of
    breath,
So they may exhale through the holes in their windpipes
The sticky flavor of death.

They whisper terrible things. They sneer. They remind me
Of their actions; of their terrible cruelty;
Of the pain they administered and would do so again —
Doctors of their specialty —
If I were not thinking up the idea of the keeper at the gate,
A silver bullet and a stake.

Fifty

Never pity fifty. All those years
Like coins beneath the bed.
Some counted like savings
With gold in their faces, some
Like thoughts that are spent
In other people's stores
And at their counters. Did you
Get a good deal?

We could not have met sooner,
You would have been too busy
Spending days to pay the rent
On futures in shorts
Or tight skirts and high heels,
Only to find the market's bottom dropping
And cellulite, before dividends.

It would have mattered then,
When your chin was firmer,
And ideas at a nickel each
Were strung like beads from your rafters
In an afternoon of cigarettes, beer
And laughter, snipped and falling
When the smoke had cleared, to slip
Between the floorboards at your feet,
Paid for and disappeared.

When we spoke
You would not have recognized my voice,
I would have been unseen
By your younger man
Whereas now, you have me.

Double Standards

I knew a man once,
Who thought a rapist
Should have his testicles barbecued
And his penis skewered.
Then he raped his ex-girlfriend
As punishment for thinking she could take away
What was his, before he had tired of it.
He had to force her down
By constricting her jugular,
And show her what kind of man he really was;
As if the association made the woman his
Table or chair or vagina.
He thought it a great joke.
He called himself a "good bloke."
He smiled at people in the street
As though he were one of them.
He smiled at me in passing.
He may have shaken your hand upon meeting
And you would have responded to his greeting.
He smiled at the sun;
He went on to have five wives
And several children. How will he feel
If one of his girls finds her lover's fingers
Spanning her defenseless neck
To do what he did?
He will wreak vengeance with fists and teeth
And punish the man — not make comparisons.

Childhood Photograph

My mother is laughing,
Holding me against the bulge
Of my unborn brother, kitten strangling
In my eager palms.
My father photographs us,
All his eggs in one basket,
Bundled in my mother's arms.

Sleepwalking

Unconscious on my feet, was I aware
Of my father's almost daily visits
As he came and went?
Did I smile? Did I speak?
Did I feel his arms
Envelop me in greeting,
His breath upon my ear?

Did I watch my mother's face
As she left us bread and milk before
She shut us in and Sellotaped our door?
Did I hear the silence
When she ceased to breathe,
Her head in oven,
Body on the floor?

My grandmother's pickaxe,
Forged in the fire of her wish
To get her daughter back,
Was buried in my father's skull.
I always thought the spike,
In piercing one, found the other
So close, the moment of impalement
Took them both.

My grandmother, not satisfied
To see her prize escape her verbal lasso,
Sent my uncle to fetch us as if
She thought we'd be waiting, as if
She imagined our father
Would release us and lose
Everything.

I let myself slip through
The gap between the floorboards
Of my consciousness,
Until the fighting was over
And the last body fallen.
But the fight just carried on
And my father kept on falling,
My brother and I tied to him
Like flailing arms.

Nesting

If no one breathed
To knock over the house of cards
Of my borrowed home,
I could almost believe
Those aunts and uncles
Were as much mine as the boy
Who was meant to be my brother.

I envied his certainty.
He was planted, complete with memory,
Beneath the bird-infested thatch
With his roots between the cobblestones
Of his birthplace. While I
Floundered in questions
Without any kind of recollection;
Even my name was erased
By some accident of emotional confluence.
I seemed unable to recover
Any part of the child that I had been.
My father, surrogate or not,
Explained the speed of light,
How to tie my shoelaces,
The numbers on a clock.

Our mother died, he said,
Of pneumonia.
Was I hers, or brought in
As an afterthought?
I never asked for fear
Of being borrowed.

I built myself houses,
With books on end across the floor
As walls for rooms
With halls, and gaps for doors,
Or sheets from chair to table,
While my brother
Puzzled at my need
To make a place my own,
A house inside the building
He called home.

Barnacles

I must have been five when I fell
On a bleak stone-bellied beach,
My hands out for a fall over ridges of slate,
That thrust up from the earth's plate.

My flesh shredded lengthways on barnacles,
The skin strings rapidly loosening
As the violin of my wrist
Bent into the blood flow.

My father ran, my dripping hand in his,
My brother in his other,
We all ran, a ribbon of blood
Pursuing us, even as we fought to escape it.
Two women in deckchairs,
Blankets over the carbuncles of their knees
Were two birds screeching on the empty beach.

One fainted. At least, she was suddenly silent
And her head dropped to her right shoulder
As heavy as a small boulder. My father
Scooped me into his arms
As if to separate me
From the river of red
That pooled at my feet in a pause,
As I leaked like a colander.

The source bubbled at my wrists;
A pair of livid corsages, and here we were,
Dancing to escape. At a hospital
That didn't take patients
The matron advanced uncertainly, with scissors,

And snipped my fleshy threads
At top and bottom.

I was not permitted to keep the strings
Singing to the beat of my pulse
Beneath my bandages,
Instead, a thousand wasps' stings
Were taped beneath the crepe which kept them in,
Their raging concerto of knives where once was skin.

Doll

When I was eight I longed for fur;
Acrylic, wool, fox or rabbit,
Stuffed with kapok, lentils or sawdust,
Or working organs and a blood supply.

Not the plastic bug-faced baby made
For little girls to practice motherhood.
It blinked and cried,
Its wheezing water-belly
Wet its rubber backside.

It was a pretender of flesh —
Even then I couldn't stand a fake.
Its mockery of skin
And painted eyes revolted me;
Its long black lashes flapped
Its lids like shutters as it peed.

One by one I popped its limbs
From the pockets of their sockets;
The fleshy plastic fingers
Helplessly glued at their edges,
The toes, nubs of fakery,
And the peroxide curls
Were dug into dirt with the rest of it.

Years later, an arm was exhumed;
Still waving, the toy corpse was testament
To my rebellion against the imposition
Of motherhood, and if the digger dug deeper
They would have found the bones

Of all the babies I refused to bear,
Buried in the mud at the back of the mind
With clumps of curling yellow nylon hair.

Food Fight

I took control of the parts
That no one else could reach.
I'd found an infallible way to get thinner;
There wasn't a breakfast I'd spend twenty minutes with,
Or a snack, or a lunch, or a dinner.
I really thought I'd be much prettier if skinnier.

There was nothing anyone could do
To persuade me otherwise;
Although my ribs protruded
I still wanted slimmer thighs.
But bone went too, and strength
And temper; teeth were compromised.
All I'd done was damage
The body of the woman
I was going to become.

Second Thoughts

There was a moment
In a hot bath of teenage umbrage
With a razor blade,
When I thought arterial blood
Might attract a mother's love.
But the mind's eye
Knew death better
For making nothing but empty spaces.

School Doctor

I shrank from the school doctor,
Balled in slime as he was in asking
How my mother died
While examining my sprained ankle.
He might have known about her suicide,
But pried away my thin veneer
From his vantage point of trusted medic,
His question a crowbar as he
Turned my ankle side to side,
Waiting, as I wept my mother's loss
Brought as fresh into the room as flowers.
I suppressed my fury at his verbal probings
As he attempted entry
Of my inner self. My anger was
A thing he wanted too much
As if it pleasured him, his touch
Sent ants marauding
Beneath my teenage skin.
My instincts clawed me back
From the precipice of him;
His vile dark eyes accompanied his oh,
Too personal breath upon my face
As he studied my reaction to his question,
As if to say "I'm a man
And I am touching you, I am, I am."
My momentary sorrow taught me
That in future visits I'd present
A show of mediocrity.
I'd be blank, without a trait,
Devoid of personality
For him to finger and manipulate.

Orphan

"You're an orphan," they said,
"Now your father is dead."
Were they just rubbing my father's ashes
Into the open wound his death had left
For me to fall into?
Or were they angling to have me reply:
"But I still have you"?
I would love to have placed those words
Firmly into their ears like seeding oysters,
But feared they were removing themselves.
Perhaps they were simply pointing out
The severance of death, so obvious,
So irreversible. Perhaps they were making sure
That I had no illusions.

Potato Picking

The old hands are three women.
I step onto the heaving platform
In front of their critical silence,
And know my place; the teenage wife
At the tail end of the conveyor belt.

We rock like skittles
As the tractor drags our lurching cage
Across the endless fields,
Gouging potatoes from the seams
In the topsoil.
Our scarves tie back our hair
Against the dried earth that becomes mud
In the sweat of our own furrows.

Our bare fingers blacken in the mounds
That jiggle and toss and break,
Exposing the pale rounds
For which we are archaeologists.
I am almost unnecessary,
Picking the scraps that escape
The other six hands rummaging.

If one stops to clear her nose
Of the silt that clogs airways
Then I might pick a handful.
I see then, how it works; the chief picker
Gets the biggest and best, filling
The sacks attached to the back of our cage
Like a queen, while we get the rest.
Impassive, she paces herself,

Her languid movements are quick silk
Caked in mittens of dirt.

But one day she doesn't come,
And her empty space remains
As a courtesy.
The next woman down is faced
With mounds of potato
That appear to drown her;
She is fighting back hordes of invaders,
She is flailing against an avalanche
That threatens to topple her.

Her panic magnifies the chaos
Of potato backlog that her friend fumbles.
Suddenly, I am the last fence
Between the potatoes and freedom
As they defeat those who don't wish
To be the first line of defense.
I am nudged into the empty gap at the top of the belt,
(This is a compliment), so now they can rest.

At night I go home to sleep,
But in my restless head
I am still on my feet
Picking potatoes so fast
They can roll cigarettes.

For Nicholas Heiney

November 15, 1982–June 26, 2006

We remembered you today,
And the life you cut out so cautiously
From amongst the detritus of
The rest of us. You were there
In spirit, in the mind of anyone
Who'd met you for one moment.
You were not blamed
For sharpening the tool
You hid from view,
That took you only when
You wanted it to,
But were loved and understood.

For among the thoughts
That occupied your mind
And with which you daily negotiated,
As if breaking through
Some endless, bloodying thicket
That just grew ahead of you
As fast as you could beat it down, you knew
You had the means by which
You could leave it all behind.

Your sister spoke for you in church,
She didn't flinch,
But read your essay on
Literary criticism being
Mostly bad writing about good writing,
With humor and a steadied nerve.

She presented you to us, and God,
In your own words.

And later in the afternoon,
Your mother and father
Brought you back into the room
Where you and I had sat one night,
And I'd read you poetry.
They wove your fabric out of memories
And the lines you wrote in diaries,
With all the love and tenderness
They have for you,
Understanding when
The thorns that hooked you,
Did so, even as you slept,
And you made yourself
The appointment that you kept.

Sheep in the Rain

Sheep bubble and mushroom from the steep bank
Beneath the hedge of hawthorn and hazel,
Bunched in woolen clumps
Against the sharp nails of sleet
That hammer and pinch into their faces.

Their legs are fastened to the ground
By feet like cloven tent pegs.
When the sky clears
They uproot themselves,
Step forward into the open green
Of their pasture, drip-dry and steam.

Verbal Warning

There are those who believe
(With their heads stuck in a can of gasoline
And inhaling deeply) that several words
My poet-parents chose to use
Cannot be re-used by me
Without accusations of imitation.

So my poems about the bird that is black,
But not a blackbird, should not name him.
All I should tell you is how
His feathers ate light like a collapsing star;
They did not glisten purple or blue
The way that other bird did,
The one I reared from a fledgling
With his black and white patches and thieving
— Yet not a thief, a treasurer,
That wanted to tuck frozen peas
Into the back pocket of my jeans.

And the long-bodied short-legged
Furry creature I wrote about once,
That was possessed of a pungent odor,
Should remain also without identity,
Although twice in my life I kept a pair;
Short-eared humps of sausage spine
With tails like hairy stumps.

Some of those things with feathers and claws
Eat long-eared bouncy bundles
Of downy hair, but not
The balls of spines that clatter

Through the leaves, sometimes
Like something larger.

There are flat-sided fillets with scales
That swim rivers and sea, those too,
Could remain nameless. But words
Are not owned; so here's a stoat, a squirrel,
A ferret, crow, and magpie; a lizard, fox, hedgehog,
Rabbit, hare, pheasant, wolf, salmon, trout, goat,
Lobster, chaffinch, pickled herring and brown bear,
     all with skin,
Claws, blood, feet, beaks, jaws, and perhaps
Preceded by the occasional adjective . . .

George

He rifles his feathers
As if searching for socks
In the washing basket
Of his breast pocket and wing-pits.
Still sockless
He slides the split blade of his beak
Along each twisted-back tail feather,
Bringing them up almost to his ear
As his nut-cracker reaches each tip.
He's as thorough as a man
Who's lost his keys.
He shudders his skin
So his black-and-whites froth
And settle neatly.
An oil-slick glistens from his bum-rudder,
Which flicks up and down like a switch.
He pauses to examine his toothpicks
On the end of which are feet.
Experimentally, he slides one forward
As if pushing a small suitcase.
Step, skip, pivot, stride,
He's gathering speed; he turns again,
High-step, high-step, skip-skip,
And he's dancing a magpie dance
To his head full of magpie music.

George Examines

His quizzical black eye
Polishes its round gaze in its orbit
As it scans everything
To the left and to the front,
While his right echoes the trajectory.
I wonder if his two visions
Are simultaneous, or seen separately,
Each by one half of his magpie brain
Which directs the careful points of his beak
Into the dog meat that I offer him.
He opens it up by piercing and separating
His scissors, and peers
Into the hole he has made
As if he might find something;
His way, his purpose,
A gold-colored curtain ring.

My Crow

He sits in my kitchen, a dud of a crow
With a creak of a beak
And a sullen eye that disguises
His fear of movement. Tattered by magpies
Smart enough to have two
Stake him to the ground
While three others shredded his balance
And his crow-abilities, he was found
Half-dead and bloodied by some woman
Who kept him in a bath for a week,
Where all he did was fall over
Between walls of slippery pink.
My crow eats and craps like a crow;
He does these small things carefully,
His dignity compromised by tottering
In between his perch and food bowl,
And the palm of my hand, in which he rests.

Slowly Recovering Crow

His heart pounds at sudden sounds
As if about to burst from between my fingers.
His claws tighten on the black leather skin
Of my thin gloves, and I can detect his confusion;
If one foot squeezes, the other slackens;
He is unable to have two thoughts together
And control his toes in unison.
He is constantly startled. The weight
Of his bony crow-body hangs from his grip,
And he settles like a feathered spearhead
In a fistful of umbrage,
His tail straight down
Pointing to the center of the earth
Where he is heading.

Armistice

Oscar is less bumptious now;
He does not scrabble to escape,
Clawing flesh that might also escape
The confines of my covering of clothes.
The punctures in my wrist-skin are healing
And he does not add to them.
The scars remain as reminders of the times
He sought a balance for himself
By gripping the nearest thing
In his nutcracker of a beak
And hanging on for dear life.
Now he allows me to pluck him from his branch
Like an overripe fruit. I scoop his claws
Onto my gloved fingers and he climbs
The ladder of them, onto my knuckles,
And sits. And sits, not moving, unless I do,
When his beak grips my sweater
To stop himself swaying. Sometimes he leans
Into my chest, closes his sparsely feathered lids
And seems to rest.

Oscar Flies

He has been unbalanced by other birds
Trying to break into his cranium
As if it were an egg.

He tilts his head forwards
And sharpens the weapon of his face
On the branch that is his perch,
Whittling a waist to it.

His intentions lie in his efforts
As he grips it like a life-belt.

Today he flapped three feet
From the top of his cage to the kitchen table
And back. This was his first adventure
In two months. He measures his progress
In fairy-steps and crow-staggers.

Oscar Sleeps

He clutches his cut branch side-saddle,
His eyes tightly closed against the dull kitchen lights.
Usually at the flick of a switch
He'd be sharpening his beak
For a snip or a bite, watching what approaches
With his critical eye.
But tonight he is not the sleek
Occasionally staggering feathered weapon I recognize.
Tonight he crouches on his perch as if beaten.
His black feathered shawl and chest coat
Rifle their layers so he looks
As if the wind has tossed him.
Occasionally, he sways and must remember his grip.
He snores gently, a little crow-snore.
He swallows and gurgles like a water-pipe crow-child
And something in his dreams disturbs him.
His sleep-talking sounds multiply
Until his own sudden crow-shout wakes him.
Startled, he peers out of the semi-dark
Of his cage as if to remind himself
That nothing can get him;
He is safe from attack from the outside.
But as he dreams
His innards bleed and betray him.
The damage of age chips away at his bones
Beneath his papery crow-hide.

The Trouble with Death...

... is that it's never one death.
The death of my sixty-day crow
Who was already bird-battered and aged
When handed to me in a cardboard box,
Was attached to the happy departure
Of a hand-reared five-months magpie,
Which was still a bereavement of sorts.
That in turn brought home
The husband who'd just left for eight weeks in Australia,
Which suggested the idea of his death:
In moments of weakness, a real fear.
The dead crow is also connected
To the death of my father
And the desertion of my mother
Who took her own life.
As I bury my crow in the dirt
Beneath the monkey-puzzle tree
And stroke his glossy corpse
One last time, I am unable to let him go
But unable to bring him back.
I almost have to rip him
Out of my own hands.

Sixty-Day Crow

So he was only a crow.
The crow in my hand at the table.
The crow resting his breastbone in my fingers.
The crow learning to perch on my wrist
And remain balanced. The crow
Who recovers from a bird-beating
Even as he succumbs to old age.
The crow who stumbled back to his cage
When set free. The crow
Who never wanted to leave.

Pheasant Running

Startled, his head rockets
To the end of his neck. His neck,
Since it is attached, stretches
Like a rubber hose. His body,
Since it is attached, drags behind
Like a bag of washing in the arms
Of a short person, gathering momentum,
Bouncing atop two sticks of an afterthought,
To suddenly catch up with the head
And astonish it by swallowing
The intervening length of vertebrae.
Now his head is fixed like a doorknob
To his feathered ball
With an expression of
Nothing wrong at all,
And innocent of the fear
That sent him scrambling.
He flutters and blazes coyly,
A mute flame, his embers
Drop into the grass.
Earnestly, he stoops to collect them.

Pheasant Escaping

It barrels improbably past the window,
Vestigial wings pumping frantically
To propel the ball of copper and green
Up, up, up into the air,
Accompanied by squawks fired from
The fleshy weapon of its panicky neck.
Terror keeps it aloft.
If, for one moment, the bird
Ceases to feel fear, then it would
Plummet to the ground like a falling planet,
Its tail feathers burning up in the atmosphere.

Dead Pheasant

It lies
Bundled like a dropped sweater
Of bronzed threads at the roadside,
As if waiting to be collected.
Only its broken wing
Gives away its identity,
Pointing ten feathered fingers accusingly
At the murderer: That car,
And that car and that car.

Cow-Stitcher

I'm a gut-shoveller.
Someone's gotta do it. I mean
The cow is fed stuff that makes it grow fast
Until it's the fattest, tightest-bellied
Thing I've seen. Then it splits open, see?
And its stomachs, all four,
Slip through the gap in its side
And trail on the floor.
Well, they don't want the poor cow
Treading on itself, do they?
So they call me in especially
To push and squeeze and jostle
The rubbery wet tubing of innards
Back into the sagging barrel
Of cow-belly. Someone holds
The two edges of flesh together
While I take out my upholstery needle,
The one with the curve in it.
It's like stitching a sofa,
Even the cow must think it's weird to carry
More than its sticks can handle,
And there's me, shoving it all back in,
So you can cut it up later
And fill yourselves with whatever
Filled it. Me? I'm vegetarian;
I don't like to eat anything
That ruptures on the hoof
Or had a heartbeat.

How It Began

There was first the small sound
Of a metal wire snapping
Like a violin string inside my head
On a long drive South in Australia,
Me, a passenger.
The sharp, plaintive note
Snagged my attention;
It was followed by a sense of foreboding
That something was wrong.
When we stopped I found
That during our journey my feet
Had become welded to the floor of the car.
I tried to lift my legs at the knees
But the joints where my arms
Were hooked onto my shoulders
Had lost their point. My man
Stared in disbelief at my immobility,
With growing fury he
Maneuvered my limbs from the vehicle
And made me stand.
If I had to die in order to lie down
Right there on the pavement
I would have keeled over,
Soulless, immediately.
Weeks later when
This flu refused to cure
The blood tests began,
Followed by a CAT scan
And psychiatric examination
To rule out depression.
They found me sane as anyone could be
Afflicted by M.E.

I could not read or concentrate,
Or walk more than a few
Dead-legged paces, or talk;
I found it hard with wooden tongue
To fix the words in place.
Inertia flooded my veins,
Set like concrete,
And immobilized my working brain.
It would be almost four years
Before I read a book again.
Now, a single question
About sugar, or not, in tea
Could render me senseless,
And sleep was not sleep
Of rest and waking, but a mud
Of the mind's making to wade through,
So that strength and cognitive ability
Were all used up
By the time my eyes opened.
The actions of a day were suspended
For as long as string. Despite my fury,
And all my efforts to resist,
My life as I had known it
Ended.

Sleep

For Lisa Baskin

Sleep, and the feathers will fall to the floor
As your wings fold, not beating anymore.
Sleep, and the embedded arrowhead
Of new loss will unpick its heavy blade
From the hole in your side.
Sleep, and the little demons will wait.
They will not drive it home again until
Your eyes open, and each day your hide
Will be hardened as you heal,
Almost whole. Sleep, and forgive it,
Let it take up your burden. Sleep,
And the chestnut will grow
Each night a foot until
You can sit in its branches
Ready again to sleep, and let go
Of the little things, clamoring.

Book Beggar

The shelf is as flat and empty
As a knife. On it sit the nothings
That I must open and study.

See the smooth paintwork
Yellowing, see the dust settle
Unhindered by any object.

The poetry books I have harbored till now
Rot with exhaustion and neglect
In storage boxes I cannot reach

In a room that is no longer a room,
But a cemetery for the frivolity
Of pages that I haven't set eyes on in years.

I am to write a newspaper column
For people who actually read. I am to encourage
The love of poetry.

I drag a dark yellow duster
The length of the sharp instrument
That challenges me from its wall-screws.

The duster is edge-bitten by red stitching
That defines its purpose. I am a poet
Edge-bitten by purpose and no poetry books.

II

They're arriving in heaps! Packages of poetry,
Gifts from the publishing gods
We aspire to please.

And responsibility. I remember the slights;
The sharply pointed criticisms
Of reviewers who write —

Who attached my parental history
To the way they saw me
And so constructed spitefully.

I look at the thousands of words
These other poets lovingly chose,
Some rightly or wrongly, some used well or not,

And I know that I'll never throw a javelin
Into the still-beating hearts
Of their chattering children.

Curiosity About an Inner Thought

Their eye-knockings
On cranial skin
Cry "Let us in, let us in,
We want to see
What rattles in that bone-globe,
What noises echo in between
The anvil, hammer, stapes,
Behind the ear's lobe."

Letter Bomb

Sometimes it does not take your hand off
As you run your finger
Like a blunt slice down the folded edge
Of the topside,
Leaving the paper bulkily torn
Or wantonly jagged.
Nor does it explode into life
If you neatly excise the flap-fold
With the nearest kitchen knife.
Sometimes it contains an announcement
Of love, or the end of love, or death.
Sometimes it brings sorrow. Or joy.
Sometimes it simply contains hope
Which might direct your thoughts,
Focus your wishes and allow
The possibility of a different route
Through the days ahead.
Sometimes the explosion, when it comes,
Is not outside but inside,
Where the real changes are made.

February

Wars go on and on,
The interminable news of the countless dead
Washes over my head as I watch
The gray sky unravel at dawn,
Then roll itself up like a carpet again
Sodden with passing rain,
Leaving only the black hole of oblivion
As sky. At night, this is the place I inhabit.

The trapped field-mice
In their three-foot tank
Are thinking of starting a family.
This is the time for new beginnings.
Last year this month brought in
Another mountain, as if dragging it by tug
Like a vast, blackened iceberg
Onto my horizon of taut, brittle trees,
And wallows of mud churned up by the feet of sheep
Yet to drop their little fleeces
Bleating, into the icy air and onto
The stern ground. I had to climb
Another rock face, just when I'd downed my crampons.
This year, older, more tired, aching everywhere,
I shall ignore such obstacles.
My state of mind will flatten them down
With the weight of sheer exhaustion,
And iron them out as I sleep into March, or maybe April . . .

Endgame

I am saying goodbye.
Our war is over. You won.
Or I did. It depends
Which hilltop you stand on.
If you want to keep score, why don't you
Count the scars from before,
And the open sores
From our most recent engagement?

I'm walking away. You're clever,
You're smart, you're extravagant
In your employment of others
In our war of attrition.
But I'm not going to play.

We've known one another for years.
We are even alike. But our similarities
Are obliterated by our efforts:
Yours to undo me or outdo me;
To make me small
So you may claim mastery.
Mine to have you listen, that's all.
You see, for me, the battle was never to win
It was simply to get your attention,
Even if love was out of the question.
I can go now that's done.

Notes

If we were sitting in a room together and you were to ask me about the poems in *The Book of Mirrors*, then these notes contain some of the things that I would tell you. They are by no means essential.

"The Book of Mirrors" (pp. 77–78): "The Book of Mirrors" is based on the idea of examining ourselves without ego. We should have the answers to all our own questions, but if we do not see ourselves clearly, faults and weaknesses included, our answers will be distorted by our vanities and will fail to resolve those questions.

"Stonepicker and the Book of Mirrors" (p. 79): Stonepicker hasn't seen herself as she really is for years; the pebbles she collects each represent a perceived insult or slight, and she will use them as weapons against the offenders. This poem is about the moment she is offered an opportunity to redeem herself. She has the chance to see that she, who believes she is righteous beyond question, is wronging others in her efforts to cast blame — because to cast blame is to absolve oneself of responsibility. (At one reading of the original poem "Stonepicker," a woman from the audience ran up to me afterward and grabbed my arm. "I'd no idea that you knew my sister-in-law!" she cried.)

"Stunckle's Night Out" (p. 81): Stunckle is born of the idea of Stonepicker's uncle. If Stonepicker is a female distillation representing women who blame others in an effort to avoid taking responsibility for what happens in their lives, then Stunckle is the male version, also possessed of arrogance. He, like his niece, believes everything is his right and nothing is his fault. He likes to get what he wants.

"The Cure" (p. 84): It has always been vital to me to know that whatever I am feeling is real, so that I can deal with it. Although mood-altering drugs may be necessary for some (on medical grounds), they don't feature in my life. When I was anorexic and bulimic as a teenager, I was prescribed anti-depressants — although I wasn't depressed. I feared they would alter who I was and I was fighting to be in control of that (which is why I was bulimic, not depressed). At the time I didn't know that my mother's suicide was contributed to by the fact she was prescribed anti-depressants which exacerbated her symptoms (she was allergic to them and because they went by another name in the UK, this wasn't picked up on). Spitting out those pills (and flushing the rest) was, in my case, probably the best thing I could have done, since I may have a genetic predisposition to some medication — as my mother did.

"Anticipating Stones" (p. 86): When I first moved to Wales I began work on my dream of landscaping a one-acre garden, so that the whole thing became a living, growing sculpture. I had wanted to do something like this for years, so the impending arrival of the stones that were the first stage was hugely exciting.

"Stunckle Goes to a Party" (p. 89): Stunckle's conceit blinds him to the fact that he makes women's flesh crawl.

"Statue 1" (p. 90): This poem describes how a child feels deformed by certain encounters, because those encounters engender resentment and resentment is disfiguring.

"Preparing the Ground" (pp. 92–95): This is the memory that caused a loss of memory — I was two-and-a-half — after this day there was a blank of almost two years. When I became conscious of who and where I was at the end of that time, I had no recollection of my name, my family or my home and, as a result, harbored the private conviction that I was adopted. (This did not worry me at the time; it was just the way things were.) This particular memory of my mother and grandmother returned when I was thirty and undertaking a personal journey into my past. I have been able to verify it, but I never retrieved any memory of the following months during which my mother died — nor do I feel it necessary to do so.

"Stunckle Sings" (p. 97): Well, he would, wouldn't he? He loves himself and believes he is better than we are — so much better, in fact, that only God is equal.

"Flea" (p. 98): When I first moved into my current home, I found it still occupied — by fleas. I developed a bizarre reaction to the bites around my ankles and was taken to hospital.

"My Mother" (pp. 100–101): When the *Sylvia* film was made, it was not in the same category as any biographical film that is made of historical figures, or of people who have been written about by members of their own family, or who have written about themselves. Our feelings about our parents represent the most powerful emotional attachment we can have in life; age is immaterial. To have them re-invented by people who didn't know them, to have words put in their mouths that they never spoke, to have strangers for the sake of entertainment imagine how they might have behaved, to have my father's infidelity up on the screen and my mother's suicide as the miserable ending to the story made me wish that the whole thing would fall into a hole in the ground and vanish.

"Stunckle and the Book of Mirrors" (pp. 108–109): Well, he was bound to find it eventually.

"Stunckle's Cousin" (p. 119): Stunckle's relative has aspirations: he is a distillation of jealousies and resentments that manifest in his ruination of others in order to aggrandize himself. He is devoid of empathy, sympathy or the desire to control his impulse to undo what others create in an effort to show that he is better than they are.

"Stunckle's Wish for a Family" (p. 121): He thinks he should have heirs, but as no one will have him, he considers usurping some other family—even his sister's—although he doesn't like children anyway.

"Stunckle as Eyeglass" (p. 125): Stunckle likes to be an authority on everything—you included—and he is always right.

"Jesus in Brugge" (p. 127): (Also: Bruges) I had been giving poetry readings in Antwerp and Rotterdam when my translator took me to Bruges to see the old town. In the square was a church that had two levels, a lower ground church and an upper ground church. The upper floor was opulent; breathtaking color and patterns decorated every enormous pillar and panel. Downstairs it was very different: the brick walls rose into low arches, forming caverns; the bricks themselves were laid in patterns and were the decoration. In a tiny side hallway between two areas of the lower church was an astonishingly intricate life-size wooden carving of Jesus.

"Stunckle's Truth" (p. 128): Pigs might fly too.

"The Idea of a Dog" (p. 130): When *Tatler* (UK) published this they put me in a minute skirt flanked by two Rottweilers for a double-page spread.

"Stunckle's Uncle" (p. 132): This is a poem about a man who has managed to get through his life to date without learning anything of love, forgiveness, kindness or compassion. His bitterness exacerbates his failure.

"Firstborn" (p. 143): In 2000 an English Heritage blue plaque was put up on a house in Chalcott Square in London to commemorate my mother's time there. My father and mother had lived in a small flat in the building for twenty-one months; it was where I was born. I agreed to unveil the plaque, which meant visiting my birthplace for the first time since I left it as a baby. I was astonished how tiny the flat was, and the bedroom in particular.

"Sleepwalking" (p. 153): After the time described in the poem "Preparing the Ground," a few months before my mother's death, I became blank (the only way I can describe it) for almost two years. When I recovered some semblance of awareness around the age of four and a half, my mother was dead and I could not remember my name or where I'd come from. The knowledge that I was my parents' child never returned, although when I found out how my mother really died (i.e., not from pneumonia as I had been led to believe) when I was fourteen, newspaper articles from that time confirmed for me that I was, indeed, her natural daughter, and my father's also.

"School Doctor" (p. 163): I recently obtained copies of all my medical records; I found in the school doctor's notes that he thought I seemed to be "an inadequate personality." I have no idea what his criteria were. But I do know that whenever I had to see him, I refrained from saying anything that wasn't absolutely necessary, and I made a concerted effort never to give away anything that I thought or felt, for fear he would use it to intentionally distress me, because his numerous unnecessary questions about my mother's suicide, when I had done no more than twist my ankle, had reduced me to tears.

"For Nicholas Heiney" (pp. 167–168): The sensitive and talented son of brilliant friends, who took his own life.

"George" (p. 172): In May 2007 three baby magpies were blown out of their nest in a gale. I found two dead and one barely alive. I called the survivor George. He grew up in my kitchen, learned to fly and, when I let him go, came back every night, ate supper with me, played with the three dogs (he had imprinted them as siblings) and put himself to bed either in his cage or on top of the kitchen door. He left me five months to the day that I found him (after two separate nights away as if to accustom me to his impending departure), and I still miss him.

"My Crow" (p. 174): The manager of a local pet center took charge of a crow that had been mugged by five magpies because it was an old bird. Crows are seen as vermin and no one was interested in fostering it—except me. I called him Oscar.

"How It Began" (pp. 185–186): In February 1994 I developed M.E. (Myalgic Encephalomyelitis), which initially put me in bed for eight months. It lasted until October 1997, although I have experienced occasional relapses.

"Sleep" (p. 187): In 2000, two years after my father's death, my father's friend, Leonard Baskin, the artist and illustrator with whom he'd collaborated on numerous books, also died. I wrote this for his wife, Lisa.

"Book Beggar" (pp. 188–189): At the beginning of September 2006 I was asked to write a non-academic weekly poetry column for *The Times* newspaper, which I did for almost two years.

Acknowledgments

Grateful acknowledgment is made to the editors of the following publications, where poems in this collection have previously appeared: *London Magazine, The Spectator, The Times* (London), *The Tatler, Agenda,* and *InterAction.* Several poems were also broadcast on *Midweek* (BBC Radio 4).

BOOKS BY FRIEDA HUGHES

STONEPICKER & THE BOOK OF MIRRORS
Poems
ISBN 978-0-06-056452-0 (paperback)

A stellar collection of poems that illuminates and explores the human experience—the joy, trauma, loss, and love that make us what we are.

FORTY-FIVE
Poems
ISBN 978-0-06-113601-6 (hardcover)

In this extraordinary collection of personal poems, Hughes takes us step-by-step through the difficult and inspirational events that defined each year of her life.

WAXWORKS
Poems
ISBN 978-0-06-001269-4 (hardcover)

A poetic wax museum in which figures such as Rasputin and Cinderella, Medea and Lazarus, Houdini and Lady Macbeth experience the love and pain and vanity that affect us all.

WOOROLOO
Poems
ISBN 978-0-06-093002-8 (paperback)

Hughes's meticulously observed debut depicts a self tested by loss, danger, betrayal, and abandonment, yet one who is transformed through experience into a world beyond nihilism and despair.